Management Projects

Management Projects

Design, research and presentation

Paul Raimond

City University Business School
London
UK

CHAPMAN & HALL
University and Professional Division
London · Glasgow · New York · Tokyo · Melbourne · Madras

Published by Chapman & Hall, 2–6 Boundary Row, London SE1 8HN

Chapman & Hall, 2–6 Boundary Row, London SE1 8HN, UK

Blackie Academic & Professional, Wester Cleddens Road, Bishopbriggs, Glasgow G64 2NZ, UK

Chapman & Hall Inc., 29 West 35th Street, New York NY10001, USA

Chapman & Hall Japan, Thomson Publishing Japan, Hirakawacho Nemoto Building, 6F, 1–7–11 Hirakawa-cho, Chiyoda-ku, Tokyo 102, Japan

Chapman & Hall Australia, Thomas Nelson Australia, 102 Dodds Street, South Melbourne, Victoria 3205, Australia

Chapman & Hall India, R. Seshadri, 32 Second Main Road, CIT East, Madras 600 035, India

First edition 1993

© 1993 Paul Raimond

Phototypeset in Palatino by Intype, London
Printed in Great Britain by Page Bros, Norwich

ISBN 0 412 46810 7

A catalogue record for this book is available from the British Library

Library of Congress Cataloging-in-Publication data
Raimond, Paul.
    Management projects : design, research, and presentation / Paul Raimond. – 1st ed.
        p. cm.
    Includes bibliographical references and index.
    ISBN 0–412–46810–7
    1. Management–Research.   2. Management–Research–Methodology.
I. Title.
HD30.4.R35   1993
658.4'04–dc20   93–14820
                                                                      CIP

∞ Printed on permanent acid-free text paper, manufactured in accordance with the proposed ANSI/NISO Z 39.48–199X and ANSI Z 39.48–1984

Contents

Preface

The purpose of this book is to help management students with their research projects. For people about to tackle a research project in management for an MBA degree, BSc Business Studies, for the Diplome de Gestion, and Diplom Kaufman this book provides the necessary information to bring the research to a successful conclusion.

The information is in four parts. Part One is on the nature and purpose of projects. It explains what a project is; how to do a project. It provides worked examples of completed successful projects. Part Two is on research methodology. It deals with how to discover new knowledge; how to test it for reliability. Part Three presents classic examples of management research. Three of the best-known research projects in management are examined closely. Part Four is on reporting the research. Once the work of discovery is completed, that is only the first half of the research. The second half of the project is to present the findings to the several clients to prompt them to take the desired actions.

This book has benefited from the contributions and experience of fellow researchers in many countries and in many companies; to them all, many thanks. I dedicate this book to my family, friends, and fellow researchers everywhere.

Acknowledgements

In preparing this book I have drawn from the work of many researchers and writers. Among those whose work has been the greatest help are:

Peter Reason and John Rowan (1981), *Human Enquiry: A sourcebook* (published by Wiley); Peter Clark (1979), *Action Research and Organisational Change* (published by Harper and Row); Alan Bryman (1989), *Research Methods and Organisation Studies* (published by Unwin Hyman); Tom Peters and Bob Waterman (1982), *In Search of Excellence* (published by Harper and Row), which includes the McKinsey 7-S framework; Michael Porter (1980), *Competitive Advantage* (published by the Free Press); Geert Hofstede (1981), *Culture's Consequences* (published by Sage); Colin Eden and David Sims (1977), *Problem Definition Between Clients and Consultants* (published by the University of Bath Press), and various writings.

PART ONE
The Nature and Purpose of Projects

Introduction

1

A MANUAL ON HOW TO DO PROJECTS

The purpose of this book is to provide a manual on how to do projects. The intended audience is the managers and students tackling a management research project, and the tutors who guide them. Each year thousands of students begin the task of undertaking a major project – often for the first time and usually with no idea of what a project is, how to do one, or what the end result should be. Each tutor begins the project period with the task of conveying to each new student an understanding of what is required from projects in general, often without knowing what interests the student will pursue or how the project will turn out. Both are finding their way into new territory without too much idea of where precisely they will arrive. The early part of the new project is most expensive in terms of frustration, meandering woozle-bird fashion in ever-decreasing circles, illuminated occasionally by shafts of insight. All too often researcher and tutor both feel that they are having to reinvent the idea of projects from scratch, as though the accumulated experience of all the thousands of projects that preceded them was not available. Proceeding with all due diligence the researcher falls into the same pitfalls that have caught previous generations, as though it were necessary to learn everything the hard way.

The purpose of the book is to make that accumulated experience of many projects available to the new researcher at the beginning of the project. It aims to show the student exactly what projects are, and how to complete them successfully. It gives advance warning of the potential dangers and pitfalls ahead. It should also make life a lot more satisfying for the tutor. Instead of starting from scratch trying to convey an understanding of a world and an experience that the student has never seen, and will not fully understand until that experience has been felt, the tutor is able to say: Read that first. Then we'll talk about it.

We begin by examining one completed project in detail.

A FRENCH MANUFACTURER SURVEYS THE UK MARKET

A French manufacturer of childrenswear was considering how to expand beyond France. The company had experience of everything concerned with clothing manufacture, but no experience of investigating foreign markets or of developing a strategy for a new country. There was no one in-house with the free time and the requisite seniority and experience to conduct the investigation.

At about the same time the company was approached by a group of MBA students looking for a project. It was a joint team from two business schools, Manchester Business School in the UK and HEC/ISA in France. The company decided that this team could investigate the possible UK market for its goods.

The first questions to clarify are: 'Precisely what question has this research to answer?' 'What does the client really want to know?' For example, is the client seeking to decide which country to move into next? If that is the intention, then the research would focus on a comparative study of several possible countries. Or has the client already decided that the British market is the only market to be investigated at this time? It is important to clarify the brief with the client and to agree on a clear and unambiguous question to give focus to the research. The client may not have thought out precisely what it wants to know. That is by no means unusual. The consultant's role is often to help the client to clarify its own thinking. A major part of a consultant's added value consists of asking the right questions.

Eventually, after several discussion meetings between the client and the project team, the key question was identified: 'Should the company enter the UK market; and if so, how?'

We now have a clear brief. Everyone knows what is to be done. The client and the researchers all know what to expect as the output of the project. That shared, agreed understanding of the brief and the deliverables should always be committed to writing at the outset to avoid disagreements later.

What information do we need in order to answer that research question?

Clearly we need information about the client company. What it makes. Which market segments it chooses to serve; i.e. does it make cheap and cheerful clothes for the mass market or does it produce exclusive design clothes for the rich? How much is it prepared to spend on entering the UK? And so on.

We need to know about the UK economy, its health and prospects as a country to invest in. Some insight into likely future movements of the sterling/franc exchange rate would help. Notice that the researchers are **not** expected to have this information before they start. They are expected to be able to identify the right questions to ask, and to be able to go and search for the information effectively. Reports on the state of the economy and predictions on its likely future are regularly published by various research institutes, government agencies, and banks.

We need to know about the market: about customers, suppliers, competitors, distribution outlets. Again various studies and market reports are published which will provide the background. To gain more precise information on the potential market in the UK for these particular French clothes, our researchers will have to go into the market and talk to people. The people to talk to include the retail buyers of large shop chains such as Marks and Spencer, Harrods, Debenhams. Their childrenswear buyers know the UK market well, though only within the segment of the market that their companies serve. Talking to customers, competitors, and trade associations provides ample insights into the market. People who have devoted their life's work to the market, and who consequently have a deep interest and expertise in it, are usually happy to talk about it if approached in an acceptable way.

This field research can be fascinating. The researcher develops a feel for how the market works, the personalities involved, how to make money in this business. It has its humorous aspect too. One researcher dressed in a formal City suit was travelling through London with his briefcase full of children's underwear. He had been visiting retail buyers to obtain their views of the garments, styles, and materials. At Kings Cross station the police had set up a checkpoint following a bomb scare. Police were searching travellers and their briefcases.

Eventually the researchers have a good understanding of the UK market and can advise their client whether entry is likely to be worth while, the alternative routes by which to enter the market, and the strategy best suited to this particular client. This example illustrates many of the critical features of every project. They are summarized overleaf in the **project plan** which should be prepared at the **start** of every new project. If the project plan is done well and thoroughly, the project has a high probability of success.

THE PROJECT PLAN

1. Who is the client? What does the client want? What are its objectives?
2. What is the question that this research is designed to answer? [*One question. Be precise.*]
3. What is to be the end output (i.e. the deliverables)?

Note. Questions 1–3 may take time and several meetings with the client to clarify. Once the answers to questions 1–3 are clear, precise, and agreed, commit them to writing agreed by both parties.

4. What information will you need in order to answer this focal question?
5. Where is the information? Who has it? How will you obtain it? How will you cross-check its reliability?
6. Once you have all the necessary information, how will you put it all together, make sense of it, and draw conclusions that answer the focal question?
7. Now plan the work. Who will do what? When?

   Start from the final hand-in date and work backwards putting in the key dates by which each section of the work will be completed. Leave plenty of slack time to cope with emergencies. Leave ample time to make sense of the data and write it up convincingly. If you are dividing the work up into sections, give ample time and thought to how to put the sections together into one seamless whole.

   Remember that the client wants one report not several bits. Remember also that the client sees only the **final** report. That is what counts. All your hard labour in gathering the information counts for nothing if the final report does not do it justice.

THE PURPOSE OF PROJECTS

The management research project forms part of most programmes of management education. In business schools in Germany the project is part of the Diplom Kaufman. For a PhD in management in German universities as elsewhere the research project is the main element of the doctoral programme and may take several years to complete. In French business schools the research project is part of the Diplome de Gestion, and of the MBA, and of the PhD. In Britain, America, and Canada the project is an essential part of management programmes at undergraduate, postgraduate, and post-experience levels for qualifications such as BA, BSc, BBS, MBA, DMS, DBA, PhD.

A great deal of experience has been accumulated in many countries over many years on how to manage a project to a successful completion, and on how projects can help students to prepare for a successful career in management, moving them on to a higher level than they might otherwise have attained. The purpose of this book is to make that accumulated experience easily accessible to students embarking on projects and to tutors supervising projects.

The project aims to get the student out of the classroom and into the real world of companies, competitors, markets, managers, and customers. The project aims to get the student out of the passive mode of hearing lectures, hearing about other people's past experiences and into the active mode of testing out the theory for themselves in solving real problems in real, live companies.

What is a project? 2

Most business schools throughout Europe and North America use management research projects as an important part of their courses at both undergraduate and postgraduate level. A typical MBA programme, for example, begins with a series of lectures to introduce the main management disciplines, such as Marketing, Finance, People Management, etc. The lectures are supported by tutorials and exercises in solving problems in each of the separate management subjects. Next the students are introduced to multi-disciplinary case studies requiring them to use the several management disciplines together to analyse and solve complex whole company problems. The case study provides practice in tackling complex real issues in the safety of the classroom. One can test out a radical or innovative strategy without risk of bankrupting a company or losing a job. Once students are confident at managing situations as portrayed in case studies they move on to in-company projects which take them one stage closer to the real world. In a case study students can concentrate on analysing the data in the case and generating workable solutions. Someone else has collected the data and written it into a sensible form. In the real world of management one not only has to gather the data and make sense of it, one also has to persuade the people in the organization in boardroom and shopfloor to own the elegant solution and implement it. An in-company project can get much closer to reproducing the messy, political, emotional art of management in companies than a case study can. A live project requires the researcher to decide what data is relevant, collect it, and make sense of it. A project also requires the analysis, conclusions, and recommendations to be sold to the client so that it is accepted and implemented.

In many business schools the educational process is in three stages. Stage One is the communication of the tools, techniques, concepts, and content of the separate management disciplines by way of lectures, tutorials and problem-solving exercises. Stage Two develops the process skills of problem solving with complex multi-disciplinary case studies. Stage Three, the final stage, takes the students out of the safe haven of the classroom and asks them to test their skills on live companies.

BENEFITS FOR THE CLIENT

For the client companies there are substantial benefits in employing a management student, such as an MBA or *étudiant de grand école*, on a project assignment. A good project is one where the company wants an important problem solved but does not have spare senior management with slack time available to devote to it. It often happens that senior management is entirely engrossed in day-to-day operational problems. As a result the MBA student may be fortunate enough to be given a project of major strategic importance to the company. A project team from the MBA programme of a leading business school should be capable of producing results to compare with the best management consultancy firms at a fraction of the cost.

BENEFITS FOR THE RESEARCHER

For most management students the MBA programme is the last large dose of management education they will receive. What they learn on the course has to serve them for the next thirty years. Thirty years into the future the tools and techniques of accounting, marketing, IT, HR, etc., that are taught today will have become obsolete and forgotten. The problems which today's students learn to solve through case studies of the 1990s will have been replaced by new problems not presently foreseeable. One needs only to consider the changes between the 1960s and the 1990s to appreciate the scale of change likely during the future careers of today's graduates. Much of the content of current management courses will become obsolete while current students are pursuing their management careers – probably before they reach mid-career. Very little of what one learns on an MBA, BSc, Diplome de Gestion, or Diplom Kaufman programme is likely to be useful in ten years' time. What may be of lasting value are the process skills of problem solving developed through cases and projects, the conceptual thinking which allows new ideas to be assimilated, and, most important, learning how to learn. A good project helps the manager to develop skills in tackling a problem he or she has never seen before. The nature of the problem may be unknown or ill-defined. We know we have a problem because it hurts. We can see the symptoms in falling sales and on the profit and loss account. The project gives practice in identifying the cause of the problem, identifying the information needed to solve it, capturing that information, making sense of it, generating optimal solutions, and conveying them to the people who will apply the remedies. Those skills are likely to be of lasting relevance, refined and improved in future years of practice.

The major advantage and benefit of a project within the total learning process is that the project is alive, active, exciting. The student is fully, actively engaged, committed – a key player.

THE KEY ELEMENTS OF A GOOD PROJECT

The practice of projects and the requirements of business schools do not vary greatly across the different countries of Europe and North America. There may be differences of emphasis. Every country requires the researcher to demonstrate a sophisticated understanding of research methodology so that the data presented as facts can be relied upon as facts, not tainted by bias or misleading data-collection techniques. The emphasis on strong methodological understanding and academic rigour is given particular prominence in some German business schools. Other countries, such as the UK, while demanding strong methodology and academic rigour, give equal weight to practical business relevance. Does it work in practice? These are, however, matters of relative emphasis. The same essential components are expected everywhere.

- *The project must have a clear objective; and the project question, to which the project report is the answer, must be clearly defined.*
- *The project must make a valuable contribution to a wider audience.* The project is not conducted solely for the researcher's benefit. Usually the project makes a valuable contribution to the relevant business community and to the stock of scientific knowledge. As a result of reading this project report do we, as a scientific community, gain a better understanding of situations which are relevant elsewhere? Do we gain something which we as a business community can use?
- *The methodology must be sound.* That is, the method of tackling the project, the method of collecting and analysing the data, and the conclusions drawn must be sufficiently accurate and robust for the readers to rely on them with confidence. Has the researcher shown a grasp of methodology which gives the reader confidence in the researcher's ability to tackle future management projects?
- *The researcher should not seek to reinvent the wheel.* Where there exists a relevant body of knowledge the researcher should be aware of it and use it selectively. For example, a researcher investigating the UK market for a French manufacturer of childrenswear should make good use of the many books and articles on how to investigate and enter a foreign market, the many reports on the UK economy, UK

retailing, the UK clothing market, and a project on a very similar topic conducted for Petit Bateau.

- *The project must be of an intellectual standard appropriate to the degree to be awarded.* It must be a valuable return on the time invested in the research. Different institutions have different requirements depending on whether the course is MBA, PhD, BSc or Diplome, and on duration of the project. At EAP Paris the project is carried out over three years in three countries. At City University Business School in London the project period is three months full time. A PhD project may take several years. Each institution has its own requirements contained in project guidance notes and in past project reports. External examiners are widely used as a means of maintaining comparable standards between institutions.

- *The project subject must be important and interesting to the student.* He or she will have to drive the project, give it much time, energy, creative thought, and imagination. That will only happen if the subject is deeply meaningful to the student. That is why most schools require their students to spend a lot of time and thought in choosing and refining their project until it has major importance for the student.

- *If there is a client, the project must be of major importance to the client.* It must be a question that the client **needs** to be answered, or a problem that the client really **needs** to be solved. No one wants to waste time producing a report which the client merely files and forgets. That is destructive of all concerned.

EXAMPLES OF SUCCESSFUL PROJECTS

Some further examples of successful projects may serve to convey a good understanding of the nature and purpose of management research projects. The three which follow had to comply with national requirements of Germany, France, and Britain, involving students from those countries and from Ireland and Denmark. The requirements of research are very largely international. Research communities are able to talk to each other regardless of national borders, sharing common norms, principles, and expectations.

AN ACQUISITION PROJECT

Researcher: Janet – An Irish law graduate studying at a French business school, Ecole Européenne des Affaires.

Client: A manufacturer of stationery and packaging materials.

Project: To conduct an acquisition search of the UK stationery and packaging material industry.

It became clear early in the discussions that the company had no clear idea how to conduct an acquisition search. Nor had Janet. Such matters had not been addressed as part of a law degree at a respectable Irish university. No matter. One often begins a project with no idea of what the final answer will be. A researcher is hired because of his or her ability to tackle new problems and to find a way through to an answer.

The client company had no previous experience of conducting an acquisition search. There were two sets of 'deliverables' which the project was required to produce. First was a shortlist of two or three potential acquisition targets. Second was a methodology for conducting an acquisition search. Once the company had seen how to conduct a search in the UK market it would apply the same method to searching the Spanish and Italian markets.

So far, so good. We know what the client wants from the project. It wants an acquisition target; and it wants a methodology, in effect a manual, for conducting future acquisition searches elsewhere.

Next question: What information do we need in order to answer the client's question? The answer is: Three things.

1. *How does one conduct an acquisition search?* Janet had never done this before but could find out how it is done by talking to people who had, and by reading about the subject.
2. *What did the client wish to acquire?* Janet needed to know more about the client's 'shopping list'. How much did it want to spend? Was it seeking to acquire new technology or market share? Must the acquisition target be profitable with sound management already in place? Or did the client company have the capacity to take over an ailing company, put in its own people and turn that company around?
3. *Which UK companies match the client's shopping list?* Eventually that question would be refined to: Which company should the client buy, and for how much?

Notice what we now know. We know
- who the client is;
- what the project is;
- the precise brief;
- the deliverables, i.e. what the client expects to receive at the completion of the project;
- what information the researcher will have to gather in order to fulfil the brief.

Getting to this stage took Janet two weeks full time with the aid of her supervisor and her in-company mentor. At this stage she knew precisely what information she wanted, and she knew how to go about getting it. She understood completely how to do her project.

Next she arranged a meeting with her academic supervisor and in-company mentor and presented to them precisely what she understood the project and deliverables to be, and what she planned to do. Once all three parties were entirely clear and in agreement on the project plan, she gave each of the parties a written copy of the agreed project plan.

Then she was ready to begin gathering data.

By that stage, with the project plan completed and agreed, Janet was feeling much happier about the project. Three weeks earlier, at the start of the project, she had had no idea how to tackle the project, no experience of acquisitions, and a lurking feeling of terror in the face of the unknown. That is a perfectly normal and healthy reaction for a new researcher faced with starting her first project. Once you have completed a few projects you will have the confidence to tackle anything. The way to overcome the uncertainties of starting a new project is to work out the project plan shown earlier. Agree it with your supervisor. Then with the client. Then you can feel confident that you know what you are doing.

DOING BUSINESS IN CHINA

Researcher: Jes – A Danish student studying for an MBA in England with the European School of Management.

Client: No client. This was a project designed by Jes to suit his own interests.

Project: Defining the project was difficult at first. Jes was interested in China. The project might help him to learn about trading with China and establish contacts with the ultimate aim of having someone sponsor him to go there. Perhaps the project might lead to an opportunity of employment in China or in trading with China. But what could he actually do as a project? There was little or no chance of his going to China until after his project was finished. That fact effectively torpedoed his first attempt at defining his project: 'How to do business successfully in China.' He could not tell the interested reader how to do business successfully in China if he had never been there. It would not be convincing.

What could he do? He did not have direct access to China but he did have access to many companies which traded with China. He redefined his project to be: 'How to trade successfully with China. The experiences of British, French, and German companies.' His project then became concerned with learning from European companies the fruits of their experience, routes to success and pitfalls to avoid. The end result was a guide to doing business in China, which would be valuable to any company seeking to trade there.

The first part of his research required him to identify companies that had experience of trading with China. That proved to be reasonably easy. Government departments concerned with foreign trade provided lists of relevant companies and contact names within each company. Trade associations such as the Anglo-Chinese Trade Association and the British Institute of Management provided further contacts. The Chinese embassies in the UK, France, and Spain provided further contacts and a different insight into the research question as seen by the Chinese.

The second stage of the research required Jes to make sense of the data that he had collected and to distil from it valuable guidance for companies seeking to trade with China; how to succeed; pitfalls to avoid. The final written report had to satisfy two audiences: companies who wanted something they could use to help their China trade; and the academic audience who were looking for evidence that Jes was now a competent researcher and manager. The report satisfied both audiences and gained a distinction.

IMPROVING THE COMPETITIVE COMPETENCE OF AN INSURANCE COMPANY

Researcher: John – A manager with the Norwich Union Insurance Company studying part time for an MBA at City University Business School, London, England.

Client: Norwich Union.

Project: The project took a long time to define. John was attempting to study the company which he had been part of for many years. In a sense he was part of the problem and part of the success which was Norwich Union, just as much as everyone else in the company. To conduct a consulting assignment for a company requires the consultant to be detached from it, to see it objectively, from the outside, from a distance sufficient to put it in perspective. That is very difficult to do for one's own company. Indeed, one of the most senior managers of Norwich Union remarked that this was a major reason for putting its potential high flyers on the consortium MBA. It forced them to lift their noses up from the grindstone of daily treadmill operations and to look at the company objectively, to see it as it is.

John's first attempt at a project title was 'What is wrong with Norwich Union?' Being a tactful man in a tactful company he did not publish that draft title. Nonetheless the humorous title was useful in the search for a key question on which to focus the project research.

After 200 years of profits Norwich Union had made a loss. John set out to discover why. He talked to people inside Norwich Union, and went out into the market place to talk to the customers. The customers are the insurance brokers, now called Independent Financial Advisers, or IFAs. The IFAs choose where, among the many competing insurance companies, to place their clients' insurance. For that reason the IFAs regularly compare the insurance companies and select the one that seems best. John asked a representative sample of IFAs how they rated the competing companies and what were their criteria for choice. John's research yielded a great deal of valuable competitive information about Norwich Union, its competitors, and its customers.

The output of the project was very valuable to Norwich Union. It identified precisely who in each IFA made the decision on which insurance company to recommend to the end customer. It identified the criteria by which the IFAs ranked and selected insurance companies. It revealed how all the competing insurance companies were perceived and rated by the IFAs against the IFAs' own buying criteria. Most important, it identified how Norwich Union performed in relation to its competitors on each of these critical success factors. This showed clearly where Norwich Union must direct its attention in order to improve its competitive performance.

That would have been a complete project in itself. John chose, however, to take the project a stage further to consider implementation. The project had identified important areas where excellence in customer service was needed. For example, Norwich Union were already competing successfully on price, and on reputation for quality and trustworthiness. They needed to improve response time. If they could give to their insurance brokers (IFAs) completely reliable information on insurance or pensions tailor-made to each individual client and respond faster than their competitors, Norwich Union would be likely to win more business. The implementation phase of John's project investigated what changes internal to Norwich Union were needed to ensure the fastest, most reliable response to customer inquiries, while maintaining price and quality advantages. The project also recommended ways to adapt the management information system to report regularly on performance in these critical success factors.

Why projects sometimes fail

3

From time to time people fail in their projects. Relatively few fail at the final examination chiefly because a competent supervisor can spot problems early. Problems which show up at the first draft of the final report can be remedied before the final submission of the finished report. There are some pitfalls which, year by year, catch a few unwary students. It is better to know about these before you commence.

TRAP 1: TIME MANAGEMENT

The first version of the final report is usually unacceptable. Only a fortunate and blessed minority of researchers can communicate clearly and interestingly through their first attempt at writing a report. For most students the first draft is a data dump of everything they have done and thought while immersed in their project. Once they have dumped their data on to paper then they can begin putting it into an order that will make sense for the reader. The problem is that the researcher has lived within the project for a long time; the readers see only the written report.

A sure way to fail is to neglect to submit a first draft to the supervisor in plenty of time for it to be read, discussed, and if necessary completely rewritten.

Obviously the first draft should be the researcher's best attempt at writing the final finished report – lucid and reader friendly. But leave time for the possibility that there may still be work to do.

As a rough guide, making sense of the data, writing it up, and communicating effectively to its intended audience, takes at least as long as it took to gather the data. It is necessary to plan one's time well in advance for the whole life span of the project, with clear benchmarks which will show whether one is on target. For example: 'Complete data collection by 30 June'. Today is 30 June. Is data collection complete? If not how do we recover from a potential problem?

REMEDY

Write the project plan at the start of the project **and** write the action plan and time plan at the same time. Go over them with the supervisor and, if appropriate, the client. An action plan states in detail what will be done to complete the project. The time plan gives the dates when each part of the project will be completed. To make a time plan start with the final hand-in date and work backwards towards the start date, filling in each of the phases of the project and assigning completion dates to each phase. Review progress regularly. If you have slipped behind schedule take corrective action early. Do not postpone the remedy. Do not give time problems the chance to grow and get worse. Shoot them while they are small.

Be ruthless. Interesting diversions have to be avoided if there is no time for them on the critical path. There will be many areas on any project which could soak up vast amounts of time. Do only what is essential to get the project completed on time and to your satisfaction, and to the satisfaction of all your client groups. If necessary, cancel all your social engagements if that is necessary to put your project back on schedule. Be wary, though, of trying to go without sleep. A few late nights and long days may be necessary to bring the project in on time. But a lack of sleep can do horrible things to the quality of output. It can easily become counter-productive.

Check out the rules concerning extensions beyond the hand-in time limit. Most institutions have some possibility of allowing a little extra time for writing up in case of dire emergency. Avoid it like the plague. A project that drags on after it should have been finished can become a burden, a nightmare, a bore. Happiness and excitement can depart from it. It becomes a chore to write and a chore to read. This is not the way to fill examiners or clients with enthusiasm for the report.

TRAP 2: LACK OF OBJECTIVITY

Before we can in all conscience recommend a course of action to a client we must first have tested it very thoroughly. We believe the recommended action is the best. But we must test it rigorously, thoroughly, dispassionately. In effect we set out to disprove our pet recommendation. Only when it has survived all reasonable tests can we feel confident about putting it to the client.

It is all too easy to become convinced of a theory and then seek out only the evidence which supports it. It is all too easy to fall into the trap of telling the client what we think he or she wants to hear. Why should a client pay a consultant's fee when all that has been received are the services of a sycophant? The client probably has enough of those already. They tend to be quite cheap.

Two examples of projects failing through lack of objectivity illustrate the problem, one from Africa, one from midway between France and England.

AN AFRICAN VISIONARY

An African student has just submitted the second draft of his PhD thesis. He passionately believes that European and American management methods are not by themselves sufficient to manage the problems of African corporations and state organizations. He argues that new methods must be evolved which draw on local African traditions and experience.

He may be right, but he has not proved it. All he has proved is that he believes it. Why should the reader believe it? A manager of an African company would want to see some reliable evidence before changing the way he or she manages that company. Another person's passionate beliefs are not enough. Our researcher has chosen examples of African companies to show that African style visionary management can work. Instead he should have chosen case studies to **test** whether it works. He should choose cases to **test** whether this style of management is the reason for the successful performance or whether there are other reasons.

When the test cases are chosen in such a way that the outcome is already known, that is not a valid test. No one is going to make a major investment decision purely on the basis of an opinion held by a stranger and unsupported by reliable evidence.

For whose benefit is the research undertaken? Often in doctoral research there are three beneficiaries:

(1) the student in learning to discover knowledge, test out ideas, explore situations
(2) managers who might learn something new about how to manage particular situations
(3) the wider scientific community who, as a result of reading this research, may increase their understanding of management.

The research has not yet provided these benefits for any of the three groups. The student has not yet learned how to subject ideas to rigorous testing. How do you know something is true? How do you know that a particular management technique will work? You test it. The management audience has not yet been shown a new technique and evidence that it works. The scientific community has not been offered any tried, tested, and reliable additions to the stock of human knowledge.

Our African student does, however, have one major factor in his favour: the subject is powerfully meaningful and worthwhile to him. Energy and commitment is essential for anyone to drive a major piece of research through to a conclusion. That commitment to the pursuit of knowledge must always be tempered by objectivity and detachment. Otherwise one risks misleading oneself.

TUNNEL VISION

A team of managers studying for a part-time MBA in London chose to investigate the Channel Tunnel project.

At their first meeting their supervisor asked them: 'What precise question are you trying to answer?' The team shied away from the question, which proved to be an early indication of problems ahead. Eventually and hesitantly they agreed to focus on a question. The question was: 'Would ordinary investors in the Channel Tunnel earn a good return on their investment?' But the opportunity to invest in the Channel Tunnel was already past. So presumably the question was: 'Had investors in the Channel Tunnel made the right decision?' Again the group shied away from that question. It seemed that there was some sensitive material here which the group preferred to keep hidden.

The group began their investigations. They examined French and British government reports, newspaper cuttings, investment reports into the project to construct a tunnel between the UK and France. They built a financial model of the likely outcomes, costs, and benefits of the Tunnel. They tested it against the UK Treasury's own model. They tested their model against various scenarios of economic growth of the two countries, reaction from competitors such as ferries and aviation, and so on. Eventually they reached the conclusion that, in their view, the Tunnel would repay its bankers on the fixed interest loans but that ordinary investors should expect no dividends on their investment for fifteen years and that after fifteen years the return on investment would be no greater than was available from other shares and investments.

But, strangely, when the group submitted their report they offered no conclusion on their original question: 'Would ordinary investors in the Channel Tunnel earn a good return on their investment?'

In their written report the group had avoided the question. At the subsequent meeting to discuss their report the group offered two replies. One was that ordinary investors would get no return for fifteen years, but that was probably all right. The second answer was that investors had been right to invest.

This was becoming increasingly strange. The supervisor drew the group's attention to the fact that their data did not support their conclusions. If they believed their own data then logically the conclusion that followed must be that Chunnel was not an attractive investment in terms of its likely return on investment. Alternatively, if their conclusion was that the decision to buy the shares was right, then it followed that they were not convinced by their own data.

The group was advised to consider the situation and to submit a second draft report with a firm conclusion one way or the other.

The second draft duly arrived. The conclusion was that the ordinary investors had been right to buy the shares. The report also concluded that, probably, no dividends would be paid for fifteen years and that thereafter the dividends would not exceed what could have been earned from investing in many other shares of only average performance.

At the next meeting the supervisor advised the group that their project was at risk of failing if they submitted a report whose conclusions contradicted the data and findings contained in their report.

An impasse had been reached. Finally the group would have to face up to their underlying dilemma. Whatever that might be.

Two members of the group telephoned to ask for a meeting with their supervisor. At that meeting they explained that the third member of the team was a shareholder in the Channel Tunnel. He would not accept that he might have made a mistake. The group would have to resolve the problem for themselves. No outsider could solve the group problem for them. The most that a supervisor could do was to convene a meeting of all three members of the group and put the problem to them. That was done. Eventually the group faced up to their problems and wrote a report whose data matched their conclusions. The final report, which was the fourth draft, passed the examination.

REMEDY

The purpose of research is to enquire into a situation about which we want to know more. It is never the purpose of research to seek to prove to someone else something which we think we know already.

Before beginning a programme of research it is essential to examine carefully one's own motivation. It is perfectly healthy to be passionately committed to the enquiry, to the desire to know, but one must never be committed to any particular outcome of the enquiry. One needs to examine one's motives rigorously. It is all too easy to fool oneself. The African doctoral student said that his aim was to find methods of management more suited to African traditions and culture. But in his heart he believed that he had already found the answer. His PhD research had one aim only: to publicize his foregone conclusion. The title of 'Doctor' would show the world that he was a man to be listened to. This was a difficult case because the student had a genuine and powerful wish to lead his people forward. He was greatly inspired by the speeches of Martin Luther King, by the books of Schumacher, and of Ronnie Lessem. What he had perhaps not fully appreciated was that King, Schumacher, and Lessem issued their rallying cries and their crusading declarations in speeches and in books, not in their doctoral research. In their doctoral research they were rigorously objective in putting their hypotheses to the test.

Research Methodology, which is the theme of Chapters 5 and 6, is largely concerned with helping the researcher to arrive at real, reliable new knowledge, and to avoid being misled by apparently beguiling chimera. Research should always be subjected to the question: 'How do I know that?'

Being keen to discover truth is normal and healthy. Becoming attached to any particular outcome, conclusion, or pet theory is dangerous and misleading. It risks killing the researcher's ability to enquire. It clouds the vision, distorts the judgement.

At the beginning of the research and throughout its progress, be careful to examine your own motivation. You should be indifferent to whether the results prove today's theory right or wrong. If you lose that objectivity you risk seeking only convenient evidence to support your preferred bias. From time to time explain your research to a friendly but critical listener, such as a supervisor or another researcher. Often the very act of preparing your presentation helps you to see the flaws in it. The aim is not to convince your listener but to tell him or her what you are doing and invite questions and comments. If you catch yourself trying to persuade, convince, harangue, or argue your listener into submission, then you will realize that you are losing your objectivity, your impeccable curiosity and becoming a salesperson for a dogma.

You need not feel alone in that. It is a trap we all fall into from time to time. Most of us realize it when we fall in and climb back out again. But a few who fall into the trap stay there and decorate the walls. Every university has at least one person who believes that he (seldom she, curiously enough!) has found the right answer to all possible problems and proceeds to bore the ears off anyone who comes within range. All things can be explained by reference to his pet theory and everything that happens is further proof of it. It is not only universities which provide a rest home for such dogmatists. Most religions, political parties and saloon bars have a few. Russell Ackoff tells the story of one man whose beliefs were strong enough to withstand any inconvenient facts.

The conceptualization of a problematic situation is a synthesis of the relevant facts of the case. Such a conceptualization does not follow mechanically from these facts. Interpretation of the facts is always present, and interpretation is always subjective, reflecting one's assumptions and self-imposed constraints.

For example, a young man came into a psychiatrist's office and introduced himself. Before the psychiatrist could respond, the young man said, 'I want to make it perfectly clear before we begin that I am here against my will. My family insisted on it.'

'Why did they insist on it?' the psychiatrist asked.

'They think I'm peculiar because I insist I'm dead.'

The psychiatrist hid his surprise and asked calmly, 'Do you know anyone else who is dead?'

'No, I'm the only one I know who's dead.'

The psychiatrist reflected for a moment and then asked the young man 'Dead people don't bleed, do they?'

The young man said, 'No.'

The psychiatrist told the young man to take off his jacket and roll up one of his shirt sleeves. The young man followed the instructions, but asked why he was so instructed.

Before an answer could be provided the psychiatrist had drawn an empty syringe from his desk, inserted it into the young man's arm, and pulled the plunger out, filling the chamber of the syringe with the young man's blood.

The young man watched this with amazement and then blurted out: 'By God, dead people do bleed. Don't they?'

So much for facts of the case.

(Ackoff, 1978, p. 89)

TRAP 3: FAILING TO SATISFY BOTH CLIENTS

Many projects are commissioned by a client company. The attractions for the company are considerable. They gain a piece of reasonably competent consultancy without paying anything like full consultancy rates. An MBA student might charge for a week what a top management consultancy firm would charge for a day. Since that same MBA could perhaps be working for the management consultancy firm just one year later the deal can be attractive for the client. Frequently the client company wants an important investigation carried out but its own managers do not have the spare time to do it. An MBA student who is free for three months may be just what is needed.

For the student the client company provides a real project, and income and expenses, and a strong dose of realism.

It also provides a second set of client requirements to meet. What the company wants may not be the same as what the university wants.

Both sets of client requirements have to be fully satisfied if the student is to earn both the fee and the degree.

In a recent example in Germany a student sought to argue that the client company was extremely happy with his project and had offered him a permanent job. Therefore, he must have done a good project, probably worth a distinction. The university replied that the company was not a degree-awarding body. The company if it was satisfied might award a fee and a job offer. The university might award a degree and a distinction if it was satisfied. Client company satisfaction would be one piece of evidence which the university might take into account in assessing the project, but that would not be the sole criterion. The appropriateness and reliability of the methodology would be an important consideration. Here there are two questions: 'Are the methods used sufficient to yield reliable information and conclusions in this project?' **and** 'Is there sufficient evidence of sophistication and expertise in handling methodology which would ensure reliable research in future projects?'

The client company wants a solution to **this** problem. The university wants to see that the student has the skill to solve future problems as well as this problem. Usually these are differences only of emphasis. Both clients – company and university – can usually be satisfied. Indeed, they must be if both sets of pay-offs are to be won. It may sometimes be necessary to write two slightly different reports, presenting the research differently for the benefit of different readers. More often the report to the client company can form the core of the report to the academic institution. The institution may need the addition of three chapters: literature review; methodology; reflections.

The literature review is a review of what has already been published in the subject area relevant to the project. It shows that the student has not sought diligently to reinvent the wheel. Rather the student knows who has done helpful work in the area, made good use of it, and progressed beyond it. For example, if the project includes a market survey, the student should have ensured that he or she was equipped with a good knowledge of current best practice in the surveying of markets and not simply sought to make it up as the survey progressed.

The chapter on methodology explains how the student chose to gather the data; why that method was chosen and others rejected; how the problems inherent in the methodology were overcome. This chapter shows whether the student is a competent practitioner safe to be let loose on future projects. It is perhaps possible to get one project right with the help of supportive clients, supervisors, and a guardian angel. The chapter discussing methodology shows whether the student actually knows what he or she is doing.

Reflections is a final chapter in which the researcher looks back over the project and reflects on how it might have been done better. It shows whether anything has been learned in the process. Where theoretical models have been used to understand the company's situation, the researcher may reflect on how well the model fitted the situation, and how the model might be further developed if necessary in the light of this experience.

These three additional chapters are important to the academic audience. Treated with care and attention they can be a rich source of Brownie points. There may be sufficient scope in these three chapters to convert a competent pass into a distinction.

Failure to satisfy both clients simultaneously risks the loss of one set of rewards. Fortunately the remedy is fairly straightforward if adopted early enough.

REMEDY

Agree the objectives, outcomes, and deliverables for all parties with all parties before the project begins. The easiest time to do this is when the Project Plan is agreed with all parties. If you suspect that there may be a latent conflict of interest or an ambiguity which no one has noticed, bring it to everyone's attention and resolve it early; otherwise it may cause friction later. One area to watch is the question of publication. The corporate client may ideally prefer complete confidentiality. The university requires that the examiners at least must see the project report. It is normally possible to reach an agreement which satisfies all parties provided that the problem is discussed openly and early.

TRAP 4: FORGETTING THAT CLIENTS ONLY SEE THE END RESULT

Clients only see the written report and the oral presentation. The academic clients examine and award the marks on the written report and the oral presentation. The corporate client may not act upon the report until long after the researcher has departed, in which case the written report is the only evidence available.

> Conclusion: **Your work is judged entirely on the written report; assisted by the oral when there is one. In other words, the written report (and oral report) matter.**

So it is a major error to reserve insufficient time to write a good report. And yet, sadly, it is an error which some students fall into every year. Some mistakenly imagine that if they have beavered hard their toil and sweat will be their reward. It risks being their only reward.

REMEDY

Put as much time, skill, and creativity into making sense of the discoveries and communicating them to the clients as you put into capturing the data.

TRAP 5: ALLOWING THE AUDIENCE TO MISS THE POINT

The report (oral and written) has three cardinal passages:

1. The question;
2. The evidence;
3. The conclusion.

They are so closely related that one leads naturally to the other. Given the question, then, of course, we had to gather this evidence. Given this evidence, then, of course, we had to come to this conclusion. What could be more natural?

And yet, sadly, inexperienced researchers do occasionally present conclusions that do not follow naturally and logically from the evidence they have chosen to present. Sometimes novices present conclusions in the third part which do not directly answer the question they raised in the first part. Sometimes, strangest of all, no question is stated. Neither a brief nor a reason for the report or research is stated at the beginning. The poor reader is reduced to searching through the pages in an attempt to discover what purpose, if any, the report serves – until boredom or frustration overcomes the bedevilled reader. In patient examiners this may happen as late as page five.

REMEDY

Write the executive summary before writing the main report. Having to present the whole project on one page (or at most two) forces you to stick to the essentials. Then when you are satisfied with your executive summary give it to a colleague to read, preferably one who has never seen or heard of your project before. Does this colleague feel that, on the basis of the summary, she understands your project? If not, you have more work to do. If your colleague does understand it, put her understanding to the test. Ask your colleague questions about the research; and do not prompt him or her with the answers. The aim is to find out if what is written is really clear. Ask, for example:

- What question does the research set out to answer?
- What answer does it reach?
- Why?
- So what?

- What should be done about it?
- How do you know?
- How reliable is the evidence?

The same techniques and questions can be applied to the oral presentation. Draft the outline of the presentation, in the form of the storyline. See if it makes sense. Test it on a willing colleague. Test his or her understanding. Rewrite your presentation until it is crystal clear to a new audience.

Chapter 11 deals with effective presentation, written and oral.

Choosing a subject

4

LOTS AND NONE AT ALL

For the student beginning his or her first project the primary obstacle is to find a subject for the project. Afterwards, when the first project is successfully completed, the researcher can see an infinite variety of possible future projects. The world is full of project possibilities. It is only the first project that is sometimes difficult to identify. Though the time spent mulling over possible subjects may seem frustrating, it is an essential part of the process of finding a theme which is worthwhile for the researcher. It requires energy and enthusiasm to drive a project through to a successful completion, driving on through the depressions and set-backs along the way.

There are a number of techniques available to help the researcher find a good subject. Some of the 'finding' techniques are predominantly left brain, some predominantly right brain. Having found a theme the next task is fitting it to the requirements of the particular school and specific degree whose rules the researcher is following. Refining of the theme shapes it into a manageable research question.

Choosing a subject proceeds in two distinct phases: finding the project idea; and transforming the project idea into a project plan.

PHASE 1: FINDING THE PROJECT IDEA

There is a wide variety of techniques for finding a good research topic. A good topic is one for which the researcher has lasting enthusiasm and energy, and which makes a valuable contribution to corporate clients and research community, and meets the requirements for the award of the degree. Techniques that have been found helpful include:

- Past projects
- Literature-generated themes

- Clients as a source of projects
- Tutor-inspired projects
- Pursuing a nascent interest
- More imaginative means of creating a project idea.

PAST PROJECTS

Each school keeps a collection of past projects. These provide examples of projects that have met all the assessment criteria successfully. With luck the project reports will be annotated or otherwise accompanied by the mark awarded and the examiners' comments. The collection normally includes hundreds of examples of suitable titles. While we cannot duplicate exactly a project that has already been done, it is normally possible to think of a dozen projects all in the same general area without risk of overlap.

As an example of the multiplicity of possible projects that could be inspired by one past project, consider the research cited earlier on how to do business in China: the research by a Danish student sought to learn from the experience of British, French, and German firms trading with China. Starting from that one example several new project ideas can be created.

(a) The experience of British firms doing business in Russia.

(b) Similar experience of French, German, Spanish, etc., firms.

(c) A comparison of the support given by the several national governments to firms trading with Russia (or Poland, China, Ukraine, etc.).

(d) A case study approach focusing on a small number of companies in greater depth.

(e) A study of the potential UK market for Chinese (or Russian, etc.) companies.

(f) Financing arrangements for trade with the former Soviet bloc given shortages of hard currency.

(g) A market study of Malaysia (Thailand, Japan, Pacific Rim, etc.) for a British (French, Spanish, etc.) construction company.

(h) A study of which industries Britain (France, Spain, etc.) should be identified as the important industries in which to develop competitive competence by the year 2010 A.D. This study would draw on the work of MITI in Japan, Michael Porter's book on competitive strategies of nations, Norman McRae's article on the same subject in *The Economist*, etc.

(i) The future prospects for investment in Hong Kong in view of the territory's reversion to China. Is Hong Kong likely to become the entry point to a vast potential market? Or is investment in Hong Kong likely to be put at risk?

(j) A number of Hong Kong business people are leaving Hong Kong in advance of the Chinese takeover. Where are they going? Why? What attracts them to their chosen new countries? Would it be in the interests of other countries to seek to attract these new citizens? How might they do so?

These ten examples, and many more, show how many project ideas can be spun off from one past project without risk of duplication.

For the readers who do not have access to a store of past project titles, the appendix (p. 181) contains almost two hundred titles of past MBA projects from City University Business School, UK, and from the European School of Management in France, UK, Spain, and Germany, and from many companies who use projects for in-company management development.

LITERATURE-GENERATED THEMES

The learned journals and professional journals are a rich treasure chest of project ideas. The learned academic journals exist primarily to publish the research work of scholars the world over. Each academic journal is conveniently focused on a single subject area which makes homing in on the subject that interests us all the easier. Journals such as *Long Range Planning* and the *Strategic Management Journal* focus on strategy and planning. The *Journal of Business Finance*, the *Journal of Accounting and Business Research* and many others carry articles and research reports in the finance area. For a pan-European perspective consider the *European Management Journal*, the *Journal of European Industrial Training*, and similar titles. Any competent business library carries a large stock of such journals, and a list of the titles they carry. Many of the major management disciplines are also served by professional journals. These are aimed at the community of practitioners rather than academics. They carry fewer research reports but are better on current practice and problems in the industry.

It is worth spending a few hours and several visits spread over a week or two browsing among the journals in a good management library. It is best not to be in a hurry to seize on a topic. Take your time. Follow your nose. See what interests you. If you get the scent of something intriguing, follow it up to see if it leads to anything. If not then come back to browsing until something better turns up. Avoid the temptation to feel pressured to find a topic quickly no matter what it is. Start early so that you have ample time to relax and enjoy your quest. That way you are much more likely to find a project that is fulfilling.

As an example of the richness of project ideas waiting to be found in the journals, let us select one issue of one journal and examine what it contains. The journal chosen is the 25th anniversary issue of *Long Range Planning*, though dozens of other journals are just as rich in project ideas. The following examples all come from one issue of *Long Range Planning* (Vol. 23, No. 5, June 1992).

(a) *The Corporate Board. Confronting the paradoxes*
   The article examines the role and function of the Board of Directors. It raises such topics as:

   - What makes for a good, effective Board?
   - How do directors strike a balance between being expert protagonists and being objective?
   - The balance between collective responsibility and individual judgement and conscience.
   - The power and role of the chairperson.
   - What the role of the Board in the next century might be, given all the changes in the environment, legislation, etc.

(b) *Scenarios for South Africa. Instability and violence or negotiated transition?*
   In 1990 two South African corporations sponsored a research project by a multi-racial and professionally and culturally diverse team to develop a set of scenarios for the country in general and business in particular. The team sought to identify the possible outcomes and transition processes in South Africa in the future. It sought to learn from country transformations elsewhere. In particular it sought for ways of assisting the transition.

(c) *How corporate communication of strategy affects share price*
   The article, a research report, tackles such topics as:

   - What affects share price?
   - How best to communicate a company's strategy to the financial markets.
   - The effect on share price of perceived strategic capability of the firm; past financial performance; credibility of the chief executive.
   - Pitfalls in communication. The risks of poor communication depressing share prices.
   - What measures do financial analysts actually use, both quantitative and qualitative, hard and soft?

(d) *Generating innovation through strategic action programmes*
   The report considers the success of Japanese companies, in international markets. It emphasizes management's continuous efforts

to revitalize their organizations through planned organizational change aimed at encouraging innovative thinking and avoiding stagnation. It is important to foster an active, challenging, and flexible climate within the organization. Many readers will wonder whether that description fits their own organization, and where they may be missing out.

(e) *Competitive and cooperative strategies in engineering services*
   This research looks at the use of cooperation with customers, suppliers, and other companies for mutual advantage. A win-win strategy in preference to win-lose. Informal networks of clients, subcontractors, and suppliers are examined to establish current best practice and to learn from that experience.

This one issue of one journal contains a dozen such rich topic areas, any one of which could be developed into several possible projects. The average business library contains hundreds of good project ideas.

CLIENTS AS A SOURCE OF PROJECTS

Some students hope to leave the choice of project to a client company. The approach is 'have research skills, will travel'. The 'go anywhere, do anything' approach has something to commend it since ultimately the purpose of doing projects is to be able to tackle any management problem anywhere. It is quite ambitious for a first project, and puts the researcher at risk of learning rapidly the hard way and possibly the painful way.

The choice of project cannot be entirely abdicated from. In most cases client companies do not know exactly what the problem is. They suffer from the symptoms. They require diagnosis as a prelude to remedies. The research student also has to fulfil the requirements of the university or business school for the award of the degree. The researcher has at least two sets of clients to satisfy. The corporate client has no knowledge of the university's requirements and no reason to be interested in them.

Client companies can be a rich source of projects, provided that the different demands of the several audiences can be managed and fully met. The advantage of an in-company project is that it provides the research setting. The research is firmly grounded in practical reality. Recommendations are subjected to searching examination of their practical feasibility as well as their intellectual elegance. The researcher has to think through the issues involved in implementing the recommendations, itself a valuable experience. Client companies also pay fees and expenses. There are costs involved for the researcher too, in taking on a corporate client. The corporate client adds an extra set of client demands to be satisfied by the research. These demands are not always easy to reconcile with the requirements of the academic institution, and the personal requirements of the student's own health, happiness, and learning. Corporate clients can be hard-nosed and very demanding. So can business schools. So, too, must the student be clear headed, rigorous, and determined in the quest to satisfy all three sets of client requirements, all nicely packaged in tact and diplomacy.

TUTOR-INSPIRED PROJECTS

The research supervisor is occasionally a source of project ideas. This seems to work better in the case of those doctoral students who have sought out a particular senior professor in order to study at the feet of the Great One. This model of the master-disciple relationship is akin to that of the Japanese martial arts student who is expected to carry the master's kitbag, wash his kit, and be reverently unquestioningly attentive to his master's instructions. In its extreme form it is not a model which fits well the management research project, least of all where the student is within a year of completing his or her own master's degree. The management research project trains the student for complete individual independence, competent and confident to tackle the unknown future management problem. It is not a training in following in the footsteps of anyone.

There is a story which illustrates this rather well.

A young man growing weary of the endless merry-go-round of getting up in the morning to go to work to earn money in order to spend it and go to work again decided to seek something more meaningful. He gave up his job, flat, mortgage, and Porsche and set off on foot eastwards. Eventually, after long wanderings, he came to the monastery of a wise and holy person. The young man sought and was granted permission to stay at the monastery. He stayed for a year at the end of which time he was none the wiser. This he took to be a valuable lesson showing him the extent of his impatience and vanity. He vowed to stay another year, patiently awaiting enlightenment. By the end of the second year his patience was wearing thin. By the end of the third year he realized that no matter how long he waited the Master was not going to explain to him the meaning of life. Finally, dispirited, frustrated, even a little angry, he decided to leave. He would go and seek elsewhere. Feeling a little vulnerable and alone, doubting too whether he might just have wasted three years, he asked his best friend and companion student to go with him.

The friend agreed. 'But,' he said, 'I must explain. I can go with you. I can keep you company. But I cannot eat your food for you. Nor can I walk your legs.' At which point our student woke up.

PURSUING A NASCENT INTEREST

A project has three sets of clients, possibly a fourth. For each there is a clear set of 'deliverables'. The deliverables for each client group are what they ideally gain from the project.

For the academic client group the project must deliver evidence that this student has achieved mastery in the art of solving complex important management problems, this problem and all future problems. The project must prove that the student is ready to wear the title and the honour of the university. The researcher is an example of what graduates of this school are. He and she can be presented to their future organizations as fully capable. For the academic client group the way this project is handled is evidence of the student's competence.

For the corporate client the deliverables are a job well done, a problem analysed and solved, perhaps also a methodology which they can adopt for solving future problems.

For the researcher the project must be a major step forward in personal development. You should be enriched by the experience. A better person as a result of completing the project than you were before. Better, more capable, more confident. This may seem like a tall order at the start of the first project. It will not seem surprising by the end of the project, provided only that you choose a project that is worth while and meaningful for you, and do not just pick any old project in order to get through and fool the examiners. Fooling examiners is no great achievement. Fooling yourself is a bad habit to fall into.

There may be a fourth client group to benefit from the project. A PhD and some Masters degrees contribute new knowledge and understanding for the benefit of the community. This original research, the contribution to the sum total of scientific knowledge, is present to some extent in all good Masters research reports. It is an essential component of all successful PhDs.

The greatest and most lasting benefit from a good research project accrues to the researcher. Research should never be a selfish activity but it is the researcher who puts in the time and commitment and who is changed in the process. Sometimes the researchers only discover this after the project. Then the researchers may wish they had known about it earlier. That is why it is so important to take care in choosing a subject to explore and a research question to answer which is meaningful and worthwhile to the researcher.

It is not enough that the project is one that a client will pay for, or which amuses a supervisor. That is not enough to justify the researcher's time, energy, sweat and tears invested in it! The researcher needs more incentive than that to drive the project through the rough patches, the dog days, and the doldrums.

The key to a fully successful satisfying project is to choose a subject and research question for the benefit of the researcher which fully satisfies the requirements of the academic institution and the corporate client (where there is one), and ideally advances scientific knowledge.

In a successful project all four client groups are satisfied. The most lasting development and benefit accrues to the researcher. In providing a service one gains the ability to serve.

In choosing a research topic, whether by reading published work or by interviewing clients and fellow researchers, the emphasis has been on finding a subject which is of interest to you, the researcher. You have to drive the project. You have to put the energy into it. You are the one who will learn most from it. So far we have been using logic, rational 'left-brain' techniques for finding a research subject. Now let us add some 'right-brain', intuitive, sensitive techniques for getting in touch with what really interests us.

MORE IMAGINATIVE MEANS OF CREATING A PROJECT IDEA

A research project is a substantial investment of time, effort, and creative imagination. It yields benefits for corporate clients and the scientific community, and educates the researcher. Any education may be considered as a process of change. It changes the students from their initial state at the beginning of the education process to their final state achieved at the end – more knowledgeable, more skilled, more able. This is certainly the case with a project. A good project often proves to be a life-changing event. The researcher having driven the project through to successful completion finds that he or she has gained benefits that are greater than were anticipated: satisfaction, certainly; confidence in oneself and one's achievement; synthesis of one's diverse ideas and interests into a solid basis for future exploration; the knowledge that one can tackle totally new problems and venture into unknown territory with the skill and experience to find a way through. We know that we can do it because we have done it.

For this reason it is wise to choose a project subject which is valuable to the development of the individual researcher. We are not just producing the tangible output of an acquisition study, a guide to trade in China, increased market share in insurance products. The project process is an important stage in the continuing personal development of the researcher. And the researcher is a multi-faceted person not just a calculating machine. At the outset of a project it is as well to ensure that your heart is in it, as well as your head.

Schools, particularly in the West, tend to be much stronger on teaching rational analytical skills of problem solving. The creative, imaginative, intuitive skills for relating to the world and to people are often

relatively neglected, although we all learn through a lifetime's experience that these skills are equally valuable.

A major survey of management education in the USA (Lyman Porter
and McKibbin) concluded that business schools give much emphasis to
analytical and quantitative skills, and too little to the softer skills, such
as interpersonal relationships and personal characteristics and development. The total process of the research project from beginning to end
is likely to draw on both the left-brain skills of rational analysis and
quantitative assessments; and the right-brain skills of feeling, imagination, and creativity.

In the early stages of the project, while we are seeking a project focus
which satisfies the requirements of the various client audiences and is
deeply meaningful to the researcher, it can be helpful to employ both
rational analytical skills and creative imaginative skills in finding the
right project.

In this final part of 'Finding the project idea' we explore some more
imaginative means of creating a project idea. We begin by considering
the different ways of knowing and of learning: intuition, thinking,
feeling, sensing in Jung's terms, associated in the Nobel Prize research
with left-brain and right-brain hemispheres. Then we consider ways of
choosing project topics, considering likes and dislikes, and working
with groups of past projects using a technique known as 'triads'. The
aim of these techniques is to discover which research areas interest us
at a deeper, more meaningful level. We shall then try out two ancient
methods for interrogating the subconscious (or superconscious if you
prefer). These latter two techniques – the I Ching and the pendulum –
may seem unusual to some readers. Treat them as fun, as an experiment
in a playful mood if that is comfortable for you. Or if you feel uncomfort-
able with them, leave them. For many readers these are already familiar
as means of working with areas of the mind not restricted to ratiocin-
ation. Finally we bring these several approaches together to reflect on
the importance of problem finding. These subsections are ordered as
follows.

(a) Left brain, right brain
(b) Exploring likes and dislikes
(c) Triads
(d) I Ching
(e) The pendulum
(f) The importance of problem finding.

(a) Left brain, right brain

Our thinking processes are complex. We use a number of ways of approaching a new situation, making sense of it, understanding it, assimilating it with our existing experience, making decisions about it. The psychologist C. G. Jung identified four styles of thinking which we all employ in everyday life: intuition, thinking, sensation, and feeling. These four characteristics combine with the two fundamental attitude types, introvert and extrovert, to give eight personality types as a way of attempting to classify and thus help to understand an individual. Jung describes an extrovert as 'an outgoing, candid and accommodating nature that adapts easily to a given situation, quickly forms attachments and, setting aside misgivings, will often venture forth with careless confidence into unknown situations'. An introvert is described as 'a hesitant, reflective, retiring nature that keeps to itself, shrinks from objects, is always slightly on the defensive and prefers to hide behind mistrustful scrutiny'. Jung stresses, however, that 'everyone possesses both mechanisms, extroversion as well as introversion, and only the relative predominance of one or the other determines the type'.

Within each of the two broad types, introvert and extrovert, Jung found it useful to identify four dominant learning styles: intuitive, thinking, sensing, feeling. 'Sensation establishes what is essentially given, thinking enables us to recognize its meaning, feeling tells us its value, and finally intuition points to the possibilities of the whence and whither that lie within the immediate facts.' Jung considered feeling, like thinking, to be a rational function since it has to do with evaluating the significance of objects and events. He considered sensing and intuition to be essentially 'non-rational functions in that they proceeded beyond the confines of rationality. These non-rational functions are nevertheless of fundamental importance because they give rise to *a priori* knowledge which is irreducible to any other mode of understanding' (Stevens, 1990).

In any decision, in business as elsewhere, we use a mixture of these thinking skills. It may be because of our training since childhood and because of personal inclinations we habitually use one style of thinking rather more than the others. All four styles are identifiable in the way we approach a problem, but one predominates. This gives us our characteristic style of problem solving, which friends may recognize as typical of the way we think. Opponents can also recognize our habitual ways of approaching a problem and use their knowledge of us to outwit us. Being unaware of our own mindset, our way of perceiving and dealing with problems, limits us and makes us predictable. It narrows down our range of options, fitting us with perceptual blinkers. With some people you know what the answer will be, even before you ask the question. And knowing how they react, you frame the question in such a way as to get the answer you want. This is a skill we all develop, beginning our practice in early childhood. By adulthood we have all become adept at recognizing each other's characteristic ways of thinking, their perceptual blinkers, the predictable way they react, how set in their ways they have become. And we use this knowledge to manipulate them. Recently I had the task of setting up exchanges of students and faculty between several business schools in different capitals of Europe. In one school the director had little experience outside his own country having established an impressive reputation in his native-speaking world. He was adventurous by nature, interested in new ideas, quick to see new possibilities. A few visits to other European capitals to meet the people running the other schools, see how they worked, and to enjoy the different capital cities was all that was required. In no time at all he saw the possibilities and approached them with his customary enthusiasm.

Then, rather too soon, he completed his term of office and was succeeded by a different style of director. The new director was equally distinguished and able, but saw the world through a different set of perceptual filters. It was not his style to gallop forth on adventures into the beckoning unknown. He was cautious by nature, conscious first of the costs and risks. The catchphrase might have been: 'I can see what it will cost us. I cannot see with any certainty what it will do for us.' For him the joint venture had to be presented as a proper cost-benefit analysis with probabilities attached, downside risks calculated, in a written document for lengthy consideration. One could well argue that both were right. Both approaches were needed. If the project was sound both approaches would lead to the same decision, as in the event they did, though at a different pace.

One of these directors was a marketing man, one was an accountant. Though if you were asked to identify which was which from this story you would probably guess wrongly. In fact the first director was the accountant, the second the marketing person. By stereotype one expects accountants to be cautious, marketing people adventurous. These two did not conform to the stereotypes of their professions which may in part explain why they were successful. Interestingly, none of the faculty at the business school was at all fooled by the professional stereotype. They all knew precisely how each director's mind worked and acted accordingly.

That need to understand ourselves has been noted in epithets throughout the centuries. Ancient Greek temples sometimes carried the inscription 'Know thyself'. Robert Burns, the Scots poet, wished

> O wad some Power the giftie gie us
> to see oursels as ithers see us!

In the Philadelphia ghetto Russell Ackoff observed a related message in more sombre form sprayed on a wall

Plan or be planned for.

We can enrich our decision-making ability by discovering how we habitually prefer to make decisions and by consciously experimenting with the wider range of thinking styles. One of the first and most shocking discoveries we then make is the fact that we only notice those aspects of the situation which happen to fit our narrow method of problem solving. In effect we see only what we are looking for. Other facets of the problem are there but we do not notice them because we are not looking for them. They do not have a place of importance in our decision model.

The approaches that we have previously considered for finding project ideas have been predominantly but not exclusively logical, rational, thinking, judgemental. At the same time we have been considering also what subjects we like, what feels right for us, which subjects we feel comfortable with, turning away from areas that turn us off, from subjects that 'are just not for me'. In so doing we have been using skills which are sometimes described as left-brain skills and right-brain skills.

The simplest way of dividing up thinking skills is to put them into the types left brain and right brain. Left-brain skills are rational thought, logic, calculation, step-by-step reasoning. Physiological research suggests that these skills are associated primarily with the left-hand side of the human brain. Right-brain skills are sensing, feeling, intuitive approaches to understanding situations. Here we may be using our emotions, our sense of colour, sound and taste as opposed to the more mechanical hard-edged style of the left brain. The sensing, feeling skills, the softer skills, and creativity are thought to be associated more with the right-hand side of the brain. The division into left and right brain, though supported by some physiological research, seems itself a touch simplistic and mechanical as an analogy, but will serve as a shorthand label.

Going to the library, reading past projects and making reasoned judgements about them is a rational logical thing to do. Considering which project ideas we like, which feel good to us, adds the complementary feeling, sensing, intuitive, emotional aspect to our decision making. It is important that we use both styles of choosing a project. A good project is both one that is sensible and one that we feel good about. So if you have been feeling that a topic is the one which rationally you ought to do but you do not feel comfortable or happy about choosing it, now you know why.

In business schools we tend to learn the hard-nosed, rational, analytical skills of decision making very thoroughly. Especially in the western and northern traditions of America and northern Europe our teaching and learning in business schools can often be relatively weak in the softer, people-friendly, instinctive, intuitive, feeling, sensing approaches to decision making. Students and tutors more familiar with eastern tradition will already have recognized these two complementary approaches to decision making as the interplay of yin and yang. In the North American Indian tradition they are symbolized as our Mother the Earth and our Father the Sun. These two complementary energies, approaches, or polarities are understood as being part of us and part of our world.

It may be helpful here to redress the balance a little by offering some techniques for identifying which projects are right for us. These techniques give greater emphasis to right-brain thinking, to sensing, feeling, intuition, using the logical, analytical left-brain style in a supporting role. Some of this may seem at times strange to some students who are always predominantly analytical in their thinking. Play with the alternative techniques. See how you feel about them. How you feel about using these techniques may tell you something about your habitual style of decision making and open up wider possibilities.

(b) Exploring likes and dislikes

A first and fairly gentle way to explore personal preferences for project topics is to work through the collection of past project reports stored in your institution. Select six that appeal to you. These are reports of projects which you consider good in your own personal judgement. Do not do this on the basis of the mark given by the examiner. The purpose of the exercise is to select six projects that you like. Now select three that do not appeal to you, which you do not rate highly. Put these three unpalatable projects to one side while we work on the six good projects.

Take each of the six good projects in turn. Why does it appeal to you? What is good about it? Why is it good? Jot down whatever comes to mind. Stay with the project for a while until you feel satisfied that you have written down sufficient about why it is good.

Move on to the second good project. Repeat the process. Identify what is good about it. The good characteristics may be the same as in the first project, or new praiseworthy characteristics may come to mind to describe the essence of the second project you have chosen.

And so on to the third good project. And the fourth. Repeat the process until you have examined all six good projects and have identified the reasons for their excellence. Note down the good characteristics as you work with each in turn.

On completion of this first part of the exercise you have a list, a set of concepts of what constitutes a good project **for you**. Different people will come up with different lists.

Take time for a pause and a break before tackling the second part of the exercise.

Put aside the reports of the six good projects. Take up the three bad ones. Examine the first bad project to see why it is bad. Keep a second list, the list of characteristics of bad projects. Move on to the second bad project. Then the third. With each note down why you do not like it. Some of the reasons noted down will be clear and easy to understand. Other impressions may at first seem less easy to express, though nonetheless be powerfully felt. Note these, too. They are worth dwelling on and mulling over. They may guide you to a profound insight into what is good for you personally and what is unpropitious.

The time spent examining your selection of good and bad projects and noting their important characteristics will help you to understand better how you should choose your next project. The two lists show you what works for you and what to avoid.

(c) Triads

From your collection of six projects selected because they appeal to you, choose any three.

What characteristic do two of these projects have in common which the third does not share? If there is such a characteristic make a note of it. Return the projects to the pile.

Select another three projects at random from the pile of six. This may even include one or two from the previous triad. Seek any characteristics that two have in common which the third does not. Note it.

Continue with this process for as long as it produces useful ideas, and for as long as it is interesting. What the triad technique does is to draw your conscious attention to concepts which are meaningful to you in selecting your project ideas. The triad exercise can be quite fun to play with and revealing, too, calling to your attention your own deeper ideas.

(d) I Ching

Chinese students will be aware of a technique for accessing a source of knowledge and wisdom which has been in regular use in China for at least three thousand years. The technique is the I Ching or Book of Changes.

For a reader who wishes to see for himself or herself what the I Ching is and whether it works, there is an excellent translation by Richard Wilhelm, accompanied by a foreword by Carl Gustav Jung discussing the oracle and why and how it works. The I Ching may at first seem foreign to a reader educated in the Western scientific tradition of the past century. Jung's comment is interesting.

> One cannot easily disregard such great minds as Confucius and Lao-Tse, if one is at all able to appreciate the quality of the thoughts they represent; much less can one overlook the fact that the I Ching was their main source of inspiration. I know that previously I would not have dared to express myself so explicitly about so uncertain a matter. I can take this risk because I am now in my eighth decade, and the changing opinions of men scarcely impress me any more; the thoughts of the old masters are of greater value to me than the philosophical prejudices of the Western mind.
>
> (Jung, 1983, p. 408)

How does one consult the I Ching? One acquires a translation in one's own language. Translations of the I Ching usually come complete with a user's manual. The means of accessing the oracle is either by throwing coins or sticks. A brief description of the coins method will give a brief idea of the technique.

Think of the question you want answered. Shake three coins in your hands while thinking of your question:

Throw the coins onto the floor in front of you.

The coins will land face up or face down, heads or tails. The combination of heads and tails is translated by means of a code given in the I Ching into either an unbroken line ____ or a broken line — — .

Repeat the process a further five times until you have a total of six lines. These form a hexagram, for example

```
        ————
        ————
        ————
        —  —
        —  —
        —  —
```

Look up this hexagram in the I Ching to find the meaning it conveys. This is the answer to your question.

If the answer moves you to a further question, repeat the process. Framing the question and reframing it in response to I Ching feedback is in itself a valuable part of the process of exploring the question in your own mind.

Jung was fascinated to try to understand why it was that consulting the I Ching could give meaningful answers to his questions, which it repeatedly did.

One summer in Bollingen I resolved to make an all-out attack on the riddle of the book. Instead of traditional stalks of yarrow required by the classical method, I cut myself a bunch of reeds. I would sit for hours on the ground beneath the hundred year old pear tree, the I Ching beside me, practising the technique by referring the resultant oracles to one another in an interplay of questions and answers. All sorts of undeniably remarkable results emerged – meaningful connections with my own thought processes which I could not explain to myself. . . .

During the whole of the summer holidays I was preoccupied with the question:

Are the I Ching's answers meaningful or not?

If they are, how does the connection between the psychic and the physical sequence of events come about? Time and again I encountered amazing co-incidences. . . .

Later when I often used to carry out the experiment with my patients it became clear that a significant number of answers did indeed hit the mark.

(Jung, 1983, pp. 408ff)

Notice Jung's research method. Take nothing on trust. Try it out for yourself. See if it works. Refuse to form an opinion either way until it has been put to the test.

A young colleague at Manchester Business School decided to put the I Ching to the test. He asked it a question, threw the coins, and obtained a certain hexagram. Seeking to test the I Ching he asked the same question a second time and threw the coins again. He reasoned that the probability of all three coins falling in the same pattern at all six throws was remote. They did all fall in the same pattern, giving him the same hexagram.

This he felt was a most impressive coincidence. But just to be thoroughly sure he resolved to throw the three coins a further six times. This time he obtained the hexagram for Youthful Inexperience, which he took to be a fair comment on what he was doing.

A reader who is prepared to give it a try may find that consulting the I Ching is a helpful way of exploring one's own mind on the subject of the choice of projects, as on any other question.

(e) The pendulum

Once you have completed the logical left-brain exploration of your possible project ideas, you may find it helpful to explore with a right-brain technique. The pendulum is widely used to locate water and minerals in the earth as an alternative form of divining rod. There are reports of its use in criminal investigation, to locate missing persons for example. Whether you wish to believe any of this is entirely up to you. The only way you can find out for certain is to put it to the test.

How does it work? The usual explanation is that the Mind is rather more extensive than the level of ordinary rational consciousness which we use in everyday life. There are at least two other levels or modes of consciousness, the subconscious and the superconscious. The brain acts as a cerebral reducing valve as Huxley called it so that we receive only enough information for our immediate needs. We actually perceive far more than we are ordinarily aware of. This greater store of knowledge is not lost but stored in memory and can be recalled to consciousness through techniques such as hypnosis and visualization. BBC television has some interesting archive film in which a person under hypnosis is asked to recall a time in a particular office. The person is asked to recall what was written on a notice on the wall on the far side of the room. The person answers quite reasonably that from where he was sitting he could not read the notice, it was too far away.

'No problem,' says the guide. 'Imagine yourself getting up and walking across to the notice. Now read it.'

The person proceeds to read the notice clearly and easily, even though in reality he is no longer in that room. While he was in the room earlier he had not approached the notice closely enough to be able to read it.

The Israeli police are reported to use a related technique when investigating terrorist attacks. Witnesses under hypnosis have been able to recall to memory every person who entered or left a bus during the whole of its journey as though they were watching the whole day's activity being re-run on a film.

Some psychologists believe that the data available to the superconscious, or Mind, is more extensive than this. The data available for recall may extend beyond the recorded experience of the individual person. That is a large and fascinating subject which we commend to readers who find it interesting. Here we are concerned only with the use of the pendulum in exploring our own superconscious ideas relevant to the choice of project.

A pendulum is simple to make. It requires only a small weight suspended on a length of thread or thin string. For a weight a curtain ring will serve; or a small fishing weight, or a round wooden bob, or anything similar.

Hold the string in your fingers so that the pendulum dangles freely. Ask it how it will indicate a positive 'Yes' answer. For most people the pendulum will soon begin to move, a little at first, and growing. 'Yes' may for example be indicated by a clockwise circular rotation of the pendulum.

Next steady the pendulum. Ask it how it will indicate a negative 'No' answer. The pendulum will move in a different direction. It may, for example, circle anti-clockwise for 'No'; or move in a straight line, back and forth. Repeated experiments suggest that most people obtain a reading from the pendulum. A little perseverance may be necessary at first for some people to tune in. Once it works for you it always works. If it seems not to work for you, give it a rest and try again another day.

You now have a simple device for obtaining 'Yes' or 'No' answers to your questions. How reliable is it? Find out for yourself by experiment.

(f) The importance of problem finding

We have now made use of a wide range of techniques for exploring possible projects. Several techniques have been rational, logical, left-brain techniques such as reading the house rules of your institution, reading past projects. Several others have been intuitive, imaginative, right-brain techniques like triads or the pendulum. These right-brain techniques are sometimes referred to as creative or weird, depending on the perspective of the speaker. Your own reaction to the full range of techniques tells you something about your own style of learning and decision making. It tells you, for instance, how much of your potential brain power you allow yourself to use. There may be some people who only ever use imaginative techniques akin to the mandala and ouija board for any decision, eschewing bounded rationality. Generally one does not often meet these in business schools. At the other extreme there may be others who refuse religiously to countenance the use of creativity, imagination, or intuition in any decision making. Generally one does not often meet these in business. For most people the full spectrum of techniques is accessible to a greater or lesser extent. They are in any case only a set of tools to serve us.

Working with the full range of techniques for discovering relevant project ideas takes time. It is time well spent. Locating a topic which is interesting and important to you personally is the essential prerequisite for a good project. Neglect this stage of the process and there follows a serious risk that the project will run out of steam half way through. Problem solving is relatively easy when one knows what the problem is. Problem finding, discovering a worthwhile problem to be solved, takes at least as much time, thought, and creativity.

Not every researcher will be equally at home with all the techniques for exploring project ideas. Some techniques may be familiar while others are uncharted territory. In that case, work with the familiar techniques, and play with the unfamiliar techniques. The unfamiliar techniques hold out the possibility of new discoveries. Experimenting with the unfamiliar techniques in a spirit of courageous exploration can show the researcher new ways of thinking. Experimentation with the new can also serve to put the old habits of thought into perspective.

Having found a good idea for a project, the next step is to refine it into a good project plan.

PHASE 2: FROM PROJECT IDEA TO PROJECT PLAN

Time has to be invested in finding a project idea. Once the subject area has been located the next stage is to refine it into a workable project.

We have an idea of what interests us, a subject which we want to explore further. It is a subject area where we want to know more, and where the larger community would also benefit from knowing more. Now we need to identify precisely what we are going to do about it. The project idea is the rich ore which now must be refined into pure gold.

The project idea now has its general shape. For example, it may be in the following form:

- I want to know what management styles and motivation methods could be evolved out of African traditions and culture. Would they work better than foreign management methods which have their roots in foreign cultures and traditions?

  Comment: A good idea. How will you find out?

- I have been working in Corporate Planning and Strategy for several years. Some of the strategy techniques which I learned at business school seem to work well some of the time. Sometimes the same techniques do not work at all well. Clearly something more is going on which is not captured in the usual planning models. I want to find out what works, when, and why, and why planning sometimes produces nothing useful. I want to find a better (i.e. more effective) method of doing strategic planning.

  Comment: Fine. If you achieve that, the pay-offs are clearly valuable. There seem to be several connected questions in there.
  - What are the traditional methods?
  - When do they work well?
  - When do they fail?
  - Can we explore examples of success and failure to identify useful characteristics?
  - Can we utilize these characteristics to build a more effective method of strategic planning?
  - How will we get at the data? Companies will not respond to questionnaires asking for intimate secrets of their strategic planning processes. A better method of research must be found.

- How should companies develop their human resources (HR) strategy? It seems to me from working in personnel that a lot of companies
  design their competitive and corporate strategies without much consideration of what people, skills, knowledge, or systems they will
  need to carry them out. Frequently the HR director is not even in
  the strategy team. Worse still, the HR function then has to come up
  with an HR strategy in isolation without any understanding of what
  the company strategy is.

  Comment: A valuable idea for a project area. One where work is
  clearly needed. How will you tackle it? What will you actually do?
  There are several possible ways in. One way is to go for **current best
  practice**. Locate the companies who do it best. Identify what they
  do. Learn from them and their experience. Create a method or a
  manual for HR strategy which draws on the best of their experience.
  If you have a paying client, you might analyse the client's current
  practice to see how it compares with the blueprint of best practice in
  the excellent firms. Then draw conclusions and recommendations.

  A second possible approach is to start with the **theoretical models**
  of company strategy and of HR and of HR strategy. Discover the
  various models available in these disciplines. Find out how they
  interrelate. Seek to build a model which combines company strategy
  and HR strategy. Then go and test it in companies.

  A third way of tackling the same project idea is to make it **client
  centred**. Identify what your client company presently does. What is
  its experience? Is it satisfied with the results and the process? Test
  the outcomes. Do they fully satisfy the company's requirements?
  And the ideal requirements?

  Next you need a standard against which to test the client company's system and results. That can be provided by current best
  practice in excellent firms and by the theoretical models of existing
  knowledge. Finally, draw your conclusions comparing actual client
  practice and best possible practice. Recommend whatever needs to
  be done.

The **refining** process takes the general ideal of the project area and
turns it into something which the researcher can actually do. There are
a number of specifications which the project must fit.

PROJECT SPECIFICATIONS

Each project must fit a set of specifications set by the examining institution.

LEVEL

Is this a Master's thesis? or PhD? or BSc? What is the standard normally required by this examining institution of this class of degree? The answer will be found in the degree regulations, published house rules and handouts of the institution insofar as they have as yet been made explicit and written down, and in past projects. The student who has spent enough time reading past projects while seeking project ideas has also in the process picked up a good understanding and experience of what standards and formats are required in the particular institution and level. Even so it is important to agree with the project supervisor what will be done. This can best be done at the time of the **project plan**, which must be clear and unambiguous.

TIME

The project must be feasible in the time available. Beware of being too ambitious. You have only a fixed, limited set amount of time in which to complete the project. Some of that will go in planning the project before any work can start on data collection. About half of the remaining time will be consumed in writing up notes as the project progresses, organizing and making sense of the data, searching out conclusions and recommendations, creating from it all a powerful, persuasive oral presentation and written report which convinces the several clients. Thus the time available for actual digging for the data or uncovering the client problem is severely limited.

Before you start, plan precisely what you will do, when, and by what date. If the time schedule looks uncomfortably tight at the planning stage, go back and think again. Most parts of a project tend to take more time than you expect, not less. Test the time plan on the project supervisor in case he or she can spot any obvious flaws in it.

The second set of specifications which the project must fit is specific to the individual researcher.

WHAT CAN YOU DO?

The project idea may be rivetingly fascinating, but what can **you** actually do about it? You cannot pursue a project where you do not have access to the essential data. In an example cited earlier a student, Jes, was unable to pursue a project designed to tell companies how to do business in China because he had no opportunity to go to China. Advice from someone who had never even seen the country would be at best unconvincing. It was still possible to tackle the subject area but a different approach had to be found.

The same problem arises where the essential data is likely to be highly sensitive, strictly confidential, or politically explosive. The researcher and the supervisor need to be confident that access to the essential data really is available before the project can be allowed to start.

We have a fixed amount of time to do a job. We must make certain before we start that we have defined a job that can be done in that time by the person available to do it. It must also satisfy the requirements of all the legitimate clients.

Be realistic and hard-nosed in your project planning. In exploring project ideas you may well have uncovered areas which interest you deeply. It may be that you will eventually explore them in greater depth long after this project is over. This particular project can only achieve one specific task, one specific piece of research.

YOUR ADDED VALUE

You are going to invest a large chunk of time, effort, and creative thought in this project. What benefits will this project create? To whom will the benefits accrue?

A project which tells us what we already know is worthless. A project which benefits only the researcher is hollow.

Before you set out on any project be sure that the end result in terms of new knowledge is sufficient to justify the time and energy to be expended on it. Consider how you can maximize the benefit which flows from the completion of the project and the number of beneficiaries. You are creating something of worth.

THE PROJECT PLAN

The final stage in choosing a project is the project plan. The project idea is refined into the **research question**. The research question is that key focal question which the entire research is designed to answer. It is very important that a clear precise research question is specified at the outset, however long it may take. If the research is not clearly focused it risks collecting irrelevant data, dissipating effort in diverse directions, and making inefficient use of the scarce time available. As the research proceeds and new insights are gained the research question may be further refined. But do not set out without one.

At this stage of the project planning the supervisor will be asking: 'Tell me in one sentence, ending in a question mark, what is the question that this research sets out to answer.' The experienced supervisor will repeat that question as often as necessary until the answer is clear, unambiguous, and an accurate summary of the subject which most interests the student and satisfies the clients. For example, a general interest in trading with China is eventually refined into the research question:

'What does the experience of British, French, and German companies tell us about how to succeed in doing business with China?'

The question for the supervisor to ask is:

'If you succeeded in answering that research question will you have satisfied everything that you want to achieve from your research project?'

Once the research question is adequately defined, it becomes obvious what information is needed to answer the question and where the information is kept. In the China example the information required is the accumulated experience in companies, and to some extent with Chinese people dealing with foreign trade, and in other people and reports concerned with this trade.

So the project plan takes shape.

- We know who the clients are, and what they require.
- We know the subject area and the precise research question which must be answered.
- We know what information we need and where the information is to be found.
- Next we must plan how to obtain reliable information. That is the question of research methodology.
- Add to this the time plan of what we will do by which dates.

The project plan is now complete and ready for discussion with clients and supervisors. A detailed questionnaire and checklist for preparing the project plan was given in Chapter 1. It is reproduced in summarized form below.

Once we reach the happy stage of having the project plan agreed by all relevant clients, supervisors, and the researchers everyone can heave a sigh of relief. The project has the best possible start and the highest possible probability of success. Everyone knows what is to be done, how, why, and when.

1. Who is the client? What does it want? What are its objectives?
2. What is the question that this research sets out to answer?
3. What is the end output of the research?
4. What information will you need in order to answer the focal question?

5. Where is the information? Who has it? How will you obtain it? How will you cross-check its reliability?
6. Once you have all the necessary information how will you put it all together, make sense of it, and draw conclusions that answer the focal question?
7. What is the time plan (i.e. who will do what when)? What are the key milestones along the road by which each key stage of the project will be completed?

IN CONCLUSION

Finding a good project idea and refining it into a good workable project takes time. It is an essential process. It should not be cut short. It is time well spent. Doing it thoroughly greatly improves the probability of a successful outcome. The process of problem finding and of refining the project idea into a workable project by way of the project plan is an essential investment of time and thought to put the project on a firm foundation from the beginning. Skating over problems at this stage only encourages them to reappear later when they will be larger and more troublesome.

We can now turn our attention to the question of how to do research.

PART TWO
Research Methodology

PART TWO
Response Mechanisms

Scientific method 5

Central to all research is the issue of research methodology. Research methodology tackles the question:

'How do you know?'

Before we launch a new product onto the market we want to be reasonably confident that it will achieve a profitable level of sales. But how can we know? We cannot know with absolute certainty whether people in the future will buy. But we can do a lot to reduce our uncertainty. We do not have to launch the product in total blind ignorance. We can run a test market. We can discuss the product with potential customers and distributors. We can identify competing products and examine how well our proposed product compares with them on price, quality, attractiveness. If we do this research well, thoroughly, and objectively we can greatly improve our knowledge of the product market and so improve the probability of our success.

It would be just as easy to delude ourselves. If we are already emotionally committed to the product – if it is our brainchild – we could easily fall into the trap of setting up tests which are likely to support our preferred conclusion. We might select and interpret data to fit our own preferred outcome. It happens. That second approach does not yield safe, reliable evidence. It does not improve our product's chances of success.

The difference between these two approaches is the quality of our research methodology. Sound research methodology improves the probability that our knowledge and beliefs are reliable, and not just illusions.

At the heart of research methodology is the question: 'How do you know?' Because it is so important, we shall devote a section of this chapter to exploring this question more deeply.

To solve a problem one needs methods of obtaining reliable information. Some of these methods, which were developed in scientific research, have been adopted into management research and, where necessary, adapted. Scientific research methods thus adopted include: hypothesis testing; statistical surveys; questionnaires.

Each of these research methods is important to an understanding of research. Each is discussed in this chapter. The chapter closes by inviting the reader to use all of these scientific techniques selectively to decide how to tackle a real management research problem.

HOW DO YOU KNOW?

At some point in every presentation of research findings comes the question:

'How do you know?'

The researcher has investigated a situation and reached a conclusion. Before acting on it the client wants to know how reliable the conclusion is. The question may be presented in a variety of guises.

Your report concludes that there is a strong potential market for our products in the UK if we follow your recommended strategy. Is that right? How do you know? To do what you suggest would cost us a lot of money to invest. You appreciate that we have to be very sure of your conclusions before we spend that kind of money.

If I may summarize your findings, you conclude that the Fitness Centre's new strategy will return it to profitability within one year. How do you know? What evidence leads you to believe that?

Your report concludes that the reason our sales are declining in Switzerland is our poor support to our local agent and distributors. How do you know that? How do we know that they are not just telling you what they want us to hear?

If we close down this business as you recommend, we put 200 people out of a job. Are you sufficiently sure of your facts? How do you know?

The report concludes that the National Health Service would be more cost effective, generating more and better patient care for less money, if the internal market system is adopted. How do we know that is correct? Is the conclusion based on sound objective evidence? Or on political dogma?

On the Critical Success Factors in this business of price, reliability, and delivery time X company is not the best. Who says so? Why do they say so? How reliable is the evidence?

It is a question which the researcher must constantly be asking.

- 'How do I know?'
- 'How do I know that I know?'
- 'Will the evidence and my conclusions stand up to the closest scrutiny?'

Research methodology serves to prevent researchers from misleading themselves just as much as from misleading their clients. It is all too easy to fall for a pet theory and select only the data that supports it.

> Scientific methodology needs to be seen for what it truly is, a way of preventing me from deceiving myself in regard to my creatively formed subjective hunches which have developed out of the relationship between me and my material.
>
> (Rogers, 1961)

The more important the subject is to the researcher the more he or she needs to be on guard to avoid getting so caught up in it as to become a crusader rather than a detached enquirer. The more important the subject, the more necessary it is that the conclusions be subjected to the most rigorous testing. One has to play devil's advocate to one's own research findings. After all, the researcher is in a more powerful position to do so than anyone else who has not seen the research so closely. Our African colleague who believed passionately that African management methods should be grounded in African culture, not imported American culture, may have been right. Or he may have been wrong in his recommendations of how in practice this could be done. If he hoped that a new generation of African managers would follow where he led, then so much greater was his responsibility to test his theories and test them again. Before presenting them he must spend much time trying to prove them wrong. Only if the theories can stand up to the most stringent tests that he can devise should they be offered to colleagues who might commit their country's health to them.

Research findings in business are likely to be fiercely challenged. Few reports recommend no change. 'Fine. All's well with the world. Carry on exactly as you are doing.' The large majority of research and consultancy reports recommend some change. That change provokes reaction. Suspicion. Challenge. People in power enjoy that power under the old regime. Change may affect their powerbase and authority. Suggesting a new way of doing things may be taken to imply criticism of the existing way of doing things, and, by implication, of the people who are presently doing them. The existing way of operating includes a sharing out of resources. The people who presently command a share of the resources may not know for sure how any proposed change will affect them. They may like having command of resources. The recommendations are likely to be challenged as much for political purposes as in the pursuit of objective truth. For this reason the researcher must play devil's advocate to his or her own research to identify in advance where the attack may come, and where there are weaknesses in the defences. This is never a justification for falsifying the evidence or for overstating a case. Once that sin is committed and discovered the research and the researcher have lost all credibility for ever.

BUSINESS RESEARCH AND SCIENTIFIC RESEARCH

Research traditions in the several branches of science have developed strong tests and techniques for discovering new knowledge and for subjecting it to rigorous evaluation. The business researcher needs to be adept in applying these scientific research methods, but the requirements of business research differ from pure science in important ways.

Business research and recommendations are set in a political context. Their implementation may alter the ownership of power, resources, and authority in organizations. People are seldom indifferent to the outcomes of the research. In theory, at least, scientific research is supposed to be value-free. Researchers are required to be objective, indifferent to whether the research data proves or disproves the hypothesis they happen to be testing. Those who have been burned at the stake for proposing an unacceptable scientific theory might testify that politics can creep into even pure science. In business research it may be necessary before putting forward a recommendation to identify who will be affected by it and how to sell it to them. In this respect business research is making a contribution to methodology which could have benefited earlier researchers such as Copernicus and Giordano Bruno.

The classical scientific method of hypothesising a relationship between variables and testing them may not be directly applicable to many business investigations without major modification. In the case of the Vienna hospital where doctors were seeking the cause of puerperal fever in the maternity wards the hypothesis that student medics were the cause could be tested by taking students off the wards and observing the results. Often in a business investigation it is not possible to change one variable and observe what happens. We may be interested to know whether an increase in selling price would affect our sales nationally. If it does and our sales collapse we may be better informed but bankrupt. At best we can conduct a small test market in a discrete corner of the country in order to limit the potential damage.

The use of very large samples to test and retest a scientific theory is not always available or relevant to business research. Isaac Newton observes an apple fall from a tree. He repeats the experiment many times. He drops many heavy objects and observes that they always travel downwards. He steps out of the tree. He also travels downwards. The force at work applies not only to inanimate objects. The experiment is repeated many times in many parts of the world. The same result is obtained. Heavy objects when dropped fall towards the centre of the earth. This observation can be labelled as a Law of Nature because it can be repeated many times by many experimenters always with uniform results. It is a generally valid law, applicable to all heavy objects at all times and in all places. By sharp contrast in a business investigation the researchers may not be at all interested in the generalizable characteristics of the whole population the world over. What is interesting is the response of a very small target market, whom we have carefully defined as being unlike the mass market, to a product which we have deliberately tried to make different from any other.

Research in business management demands sophisticated technique from its explorers because of the significance of its outcomes and because of the special nature of the situations it has to investigate. A competent researcher or consultant in business management must have a very sophisticated knowledge of research methodology across a broad range of science, plus advanced skill in applying good research methodology to the special context of business organizations.

Techniques which have their origins in the physical sciences and which can be usefully adapted to management research include hypothesis testing, also known as experimental research, and the statistical analysis to identify relationships. Much of the statistical analysis work to be found in management research is applied to data elicited by way of questionnaires. Each of these techniques is considered separately in the following pages. The social sciences, and particularly management research, are developing a range of techniques designed to improve our knowledge and understanding of people, of organizations, and of management. Notable among these are qualitative research techniques such as action research, process consulting, and endogenous research, all of which are discussed in the following chapters.

These research methods are presented for their usefulness to the practising manager. Most people reading this book are already managers or in training for future careers as managers. Not many see their future careers entirely as academic researchers. For that reason research methods are discussed from the point of view of their contribution towards enabling managers to manage more effectively. The research techniques discussed here are designed to help practising managers understand and manage the new and unfamiliar situations they will encounter in the future. References at the end of the book identify valuable works devoted entirely to methodology for readers who wish to pursue the subject further.

The scientific methods most commonly adopted into business research are:

- Hypothesis testing
- Statistical surveys
- Questionnaires.

Each is discussed in turn in the following pages from the point of view of its relevance to management research.

Hypothesis testing, also known as experimental research, is central to an understanding of research method. It consists of observing a situation to try to discover what elements of the situation cause what effects. When we think we have identified a possible causal relationship we then set up an experiment to test it. One of the classic examples of the experimental research method occurred at the Vienna hospital at the turn of the century. High mortality rates were occurring in one maternity ward but not in the other. The researchers observed both wards in the hope of discovering the cause. They noticed a number of possible causes and set up experiments to test them. One possible cause of the different mortality rates on the two wards was that medical students worked on one ward, not on the other. Could this be the cause?

An experiment was set up to test whether this was the cause. The students were taken off the wards. The researchers observed to see if the mortality rate fell. Nothing changed. It was therefore concluded that students were not the cause of death. Other causes must be sought.

The Vienna hospital case is such a classic example of a hypothesis testing approach to research methodology that it is worth examining in detail. It exhibits many of the key characteristics of experimental design.

In fairness to the Vienna hospital it should be noted that all this happened a long time ago before pathology, hygiene, and the transmission of diseases were well understood anywhere.

HYPOTHESIS TESTING

The case of the Vienna hospital is a classical example of research methodology as hypothesis testing.

At the Vienna hospital there were two maternity wards. More mothers died in Ward A than in Ward B. The objective of the research was to discover the causes of the higher death rate in Ward A.

Here we have a clear research objective. The research has clear value: lives may be saved. There is a population to be tested, the test group, and another similar population with which to compare it. For the purpose of the research it was first necessary to ensure that the two populations were comparable; that there were no significant differences between the groups of women put into each ward that could account for the different mortality rates. It was necessary to check that Ward B patients were not all from affluent, well-fed suburbs, and that Ward A patients were not all from poor areas with lower life expectancy. Investigation showed that the two populations, the test group Ward A and the control group Ward B, were entirely comparable in every respect before entering hospital.

The only observable difference was that more Ward A patients died. The selection of which women went into which ward was done on a random basis.

The researchers studied the two wards to try to discover differences that might account for the different mortality rates. They observed that medical students worked on Ward A, but not on Ward B. Might that be the cause?

Here we have the first hypothesis:

H1: *Medical students* (the independent variable) *lead to higher mortality rates* (the dependent variable).

The dependent variable is so called because it depends on some other factor. The independent variable does not depend on anything.

Having specified the hypothesis, the independent and dependent variables, and the causal relationship between them, the researchers could proceed to test Hypothesis One.

They removed the medical students from Ward A. They observed mortality rates on both wards to see if Ward A rates dropped to Ward B levels. No change was observed. Ward A still had a higher mortality rate. The researchers concluded that medical students were not the cause. The first hypothesis (H1) was disproved.

Other possible causes were sought. It was observed that the priest passed through Ward A on his way to give the last rites to dying patients. He did not pass through Ward B because of the physical layout of the hospital. This observation led to the second hypothesis:

H2: *Did the sight of the priest lead to the higher mortality rate?*

The priest was banned from passing through the wards. No change was observed in death rates. Ward A continued to bury more patients than Ward B. The second hypothesis (H2) was proved false.

Several other hypotheses were tested. Eventually it was observed that the senior medical professors attended Ward A after working in autopsy. They did not attend Ward B after autopsies. They attended Ward B on different days because of their work routines. This led to the hypothesis that the professors somehow carried the fever from the autopsy room to the delivery ward. The hypothesis was tested by stopping the professors from doing autopsies and deliveries on the same day. Mortality rates on Ward A dropped to the levels of Ward B. The cause was identified.

Several features of the Vienna hospital case are remarkable. It exhibits clearly the main characteristics of the hypothesis testing method of research: test group, control group, hypothesis, dependent variable, independent variable, hypothesized causal relationship, test by changing the independent variable and observe for a change in the dependent variable.

The case also draws attention to the ethical questions of research. The hypothesis testing took years to complete. During that time many Ward A patients died. Might they not have died if Ward A had been closed immediately the higher death rate was discovered? It may be argued in defence of the hospital that the cause of death would not have been known. It might even have transferred to Ward B, perhaps. Once the cause of death was known all other hospitals could learn from it, thus perhaps saving other lives. Whether Ward A patients and their relatives would have been content to know that they had died in the interests of science is nowhere recorded. They were not informed.

That raises a second ethical question. Was it ethical not to inform patients that by entering Ward A they were increasing their risk of dying? The patients were unknowing variables in an experiment with their lives. The dependent variable was their death rate.

There are few opportunities in business to apply such a hypothesis test in its pure form. The movement of company shares quoted on a stock market is one of the relatively few examples. Changes in an independent variable – for example, earnings per share or dividend – can be compared with changes in the dependent variable, the share price, to see if there is a correlation which might signify cause and effect. Share price movements are a rich field for hypothesis testing because there is a very large population – the daily and hourly movements in the prices of thousands of companies' shares – and a limited number of directly observable variables, such as dividend, earnings per share, for each company share. In such helpful circumstances it is possible to test the effect which interesting variables have on the share prices generally. By contrast, a company wishing to predict how sales of its product might be affected by a change in selling price or in advertising support has very little evidence to draw on. Management is not in a position to change price weekly in order to monitor the effect on sales. Arnold Weinstock, chairman of GEC, is quoted as saying: 'I know that half the money we spend on advertising is wasted. The problem is that I do not know which half.' This is a mixed blessing for advertising agencies. It is not generally possible to prove to clients that increasing their advertising budget necessarily leads to increased sales. In good times it is easier for the agency to point to how much the client's competitors are spending. In bad times advertising budgets are among the first to be cut. Still the agencies cannot prove that a cut in the advertising budget will lead to a cut in sales.

In its general form, hypothesis testing can be described as

$$H: \triangle IV \rightarrow \triangle DV$$

that is, a change in the independent variable ($\triangle IV$) causes a change in the dependent variable ($\triangle DV$). The Vienna hospital case follows that precise format.

H1, the first hypothesis, was that medical students were the cause of the higher mortality rates in Ward A. Therefore the test is: change the independent variable, i.e. remove the students. Observe to see if there is a change in the dependent variable, i.e. the mortality rate in Ward A. There is not, the hypothesis is disproved.

Notice the importance of the control group. The control group Ward B is exactly the same as Ward A except in two respects: the dependent variable, the mortality rate, and the independent variable which we change only in Ward A. If we only had Ward A and no control group we could not be so sure that the change in the dependent variable was caused by the change in the independent variable. It might have been caused by some other change which happened at the same time unbeknown to the researchers. Suppose, for example, the Vienna researchers remove medical students from the ward and mortality rates drop. Does this prove that removal of the students was the cause of the decrease in death rate? There may be other causes. For example, there may have been an increase in vaccinations against the fever. In that case the mortality rates in both wards might be expected to drop. Or the incidence of the fever may follow some seasonal pattern. Again this would affect the control group, Ward B, as well as the test group, Ward A. Without a control group we cannot be sure that the change in the dependent variable (the death rate in Ward A) is caused by the change in the independent variable. At this point the astute reader may exclaim: 'Ah! But you can test it! Put the students back on the ward. See if death rates go up. Then take the students off the ward. See if death rates come down. Repeat that a few times. See if the correlation holds good.'

Can we really do that? Knowing, or at least suspecting, that we have found the possible cause of death, can we put it back in contact with the patients to see if it kills them? And if it does, can we repeat the experiment several times just to make sure we have got it right? For ethical reasons that test is not available to us. Thanks to the control group we do not need it.

In the case of a company wishing to test the effectiveness of its advertising in increasing sales, hypothesis testing in its simple form may not be available. Let us try to establish *why* it is not available. The hypothesis is:

An increase in advertising spend (IV) *causes an increase in sales* (DV).

There is no control group. So if sales increase we do not know whether this was because of the increase in advertising spend or whether the sales increase would have happened anyway for some other unspecified reason.

The option is always open to us to move advertising spend up and down several times to see what effect this may have. But we may not like the effect it has. Dropping our advertising spend may damage our sales, especially if competitors seize the opportunity to boost their advertising and capture our market share. If that does suggest a correlation we would be unlikely to want to repeat it just to make sure. The effect may be time-lagged. When sales change we do not know whether they are responding to our latest change in advertising, or to the change we made six months ago, or to an increase in the competitors' selling price. Economics ministers face the same problem on a horrendous scale in trying to manage the national economy. That system has very many variables, many of which are probably interconnected in ways that are not understood, some of which are time-lagged on different time-scales, and are outside the ministers' control. With such a complex and ill-understood system, a question such as 'Will a cut in income tax cause a rise in inflation?' becomes almost ludicrously funny. The answer is: 'Yes it probably will but we do not know when and by that time several dozen other factors, most of which we do not control, will also have affected it, in ways we cannot foretell.'

Faced with these problems the management researcher has to proceed with caution and thoughtfulness. Specifying one's hypotheses is always a worthwhile exercise in clarifying the researcher's own thinking. The people in the company who have been working with the problem area for years have gained useful experience and have formed their own ideas of working relationships. Their hypotheses, expressed or implied, can give valuable insights and clues into how a system works. Their hypotheses, the way they habitually make sense of their world, are a major cause of their behaviour and are therefore important to understand.

It may be possible to check hypotheses to a limited extent, even where full proof is not possible. Test markets and small samples, for example, may not tell us for certain whether a new product will sell well, but they can help us improve our chances. In the example cited earlier of testing the effectiveness of advertising on increasing sales, it may not be possible to prove a certain cause and effect. But nonetheless we can do a lot better than a shot in the dark. The people working in the market and with similar products have accumulated a wealth of relevant knowledge and experience. Carefully selected and rigorously observed test markets can tell us a lot. They can certainly help us to avoid backing an obvious loser. Competing products have established a track record which offers us insights into performance in the market. The researcher who understands the rigorous methods of scientific research and can add the skill and street wisdom to find relevant information in an uncertain political, competitive environment can achieve a great deal more than someone who has neither set of skills, or only one.

STATISTICAL SURVEYS

A second research technique which the management researcher may find useful is the statistical survey.

Statistical surveys work on the assumption that in a large homogeneous population the behaviour and characteristics of the total population can be predicted by observing the behaviour of a smaller representative sample drawn from that total population.

That similarity between the larger population and the smaller sample drawn from it has obvious relevance to business research. A car manufacturer, for example, wishes to know whether a proposed new model will sell in sufficient numbers at a given price to make it economically viable. To ask every one of the potential customers their opinion would be prohibitively expensive. But that may not be necessary. Provided that a smaller sample can be found that has the same characteristics as the total population from which it is drawn, information about the smaller sample can be used to draw inferences about the total population. In this way we may not need to know what all ten million car buyers in France think about a proposed new model. The opinions of one thousand will be sufficient provided that they are truly representative of the ten million from which they are drawn. If it were true then it would be wonderfully convenient, a sound reason for treating the theory with suspicion. The car manufacturer could deduce that since 26% of the representative sample wish to purchase the cars, 26% of the ten million target population will also wish to buy the cars. This would allow the manufacturer to calculate how many cars to produce and what the profit should be. In practice it does not work out quite like that. Manufacturers do indeed make statistical surveys of representative samples and seek to draw from them inferences about larger populations. But they do not base their investment decision only on such uncorroborated data.

Opinion polls work in this way. Pollsters claim to be able to predict how an entire country will vote simply by asking a thousand people for their voting intentions. Opinion polls in Britain were treated with a certain scepticism after the 1992 General Election. Large numbers of opinion polls consistently predicted a small Labour winning majority. At the election Labour lost by a substantial majority. Pollsters and Party have since been inquiring into how they got it so wrong. Many things may have gone wrong with the surveys. The sample may not have been truly representative of the population at large. People may not have told the pollsters the truth about their voting intentions. They may have changed their minds. The poll predictions may even have influenced people's voting in the real election. In France opinion polls are banned in the final week before a General Election to avoid the possibility of polls affecting voting.

Statistical surveys have a relevance in market research. Questionnaires can be used as a relatively cheap way of asking a large number of people about their purchasing preferences. But the design of the questionnaire is all-important. For example, recently it has been difficult to pass through Heathrow Airport without being approached by a survey researcher with questions such as

Did you find the cabin crew
a. helpful?
b. unhelpful?
c. indifferent?

Sadly there is no space in which to reply 'I couldn't give a stuff about the cabin crew. I'm only on this flight because my seat on the plane three hours earlier was double booked and I had to wait.' The customer is not explaining what is expected from an airline, but is instead being permitted only to select one of three alternative responses which the surveyors have pre-selected. The result may fail to give any deep insight into customers' real reasons for selecting an airline.

This style of statistical survey research does allow producers to claim that

- 91% of all railway trains run on time
- 8 out of 10 cats prefer Wizzo cat food (later amended coyly to '8 out of 10 cats whose owners expressed a preference said they preferred Wizzo').

Statistical analysis of a large series of data over a long period of time can discover whether there is a relationship between two events or observations. What that relationship is we may not yet be able to say. But the observation that the occurrence of one event seems to be linked with the occurrence of another event sets us searching to uncover the nature of the relationship. Detailed study of the lifestyles of a very large number of cancer patients over many years led to the discovery of a correlation between smoking and lung cancer. Once this correlation had been noticed researchers were directed to examine time series data on other populations of lung cancer victims. The correlation was present in those populations, too. The correlation is not as strong as event A causes event B as in the Vienna hospital case. Rather the relationship seems to be smoking increases the risk of lung cancer. Experimental research to test the hypothesis that smoking causes lung cancer is not possible on ethical grounds. It would require that people or animals be made to smoke cigarettes to see if they contracted the disease. The power of the statistical analysis lies in the fact that by observing data on the populations which we have tested, we are able to make predictions about other populations which we have not tested.

In physical science research the statistical analysis of large samples of homogeneous data can be a powerful tool for understanding causal relationships. Weather patterns are one good example where thousands of hourly observations from all over the world and above it in space are collected and fed into computer models which try to discover predictive patterns. The pay-off for being able to predict the weather is enormous, for agriculture in the Americas and for flood warnings in Bangladesh. Some progress in predicting weather patterns some distance into the future has been possible, even though the exact relationships between all the variables are not fully understood. Our models of the global weather system are not completely reliable or accurate. The relatively new science of Chaos Theory is beginning to offer some understanding of why this may be so. Even though we do not understand the full causal relationship between one weather pattern and another, we can observe that on a large number of occasions one particular weather pattern, say a depression in the Azores, tends to be followed some days later by high tides on the Bangladesh coasts.

Large-scale statistically analysed data has established a clear correlation between smoking and cancer; between obesity and heart attack; between owning a pet cat or dog and recovery from a mild heart attack. All these discoveries and many others stem from statistical analysis of very large populations of data which indicate that the existence of event A increases the probability of event B. Event A, smoking 20 cigarettes per day, increases the probability of death from lung cancer by x% by age y years. The statement is probabilistic, not definite. One cannot say that a person who smokes will get cancer. One can say only that the probability is increased. Current research allows that probability to be estimated. Given a large population, say ten thousand smokers, the research does predict the number that will contract cancer. It cannot predict who they will be. This notion of a probability distribution related to large numbers can be easily put to the test. Toss a coin once and one has no idea which way it will land, heads or tails. Either is equally probable. But toss the coin ten times and one can be reasonably sure that it will land face up approximately five times, tail up approximately five times. Increase the number of throws to one hundred and the probability distribution will be very close to fifty-fifty. Observing the probability distribution for one hundred throws allows us to make confident predictions about what will happen if we make a further one thousand throws. The same probability distribution in the smaller sample will recur in the larger sample, provided all other conditions remain unchanged. While this may seem delightfully obvious, it should nonetheless be noted that we are in fact predicting the future.

The underlying philosophy which allows us to make such predictions is quite interesting. It assumes that the world operates to a pattern. The pattern is assumed to be probabilistic. It assumes that the pattern in a large sample is also contained in a small sample taken from that larger sample, provided that we take care not to falsify the logic by selecting an unrepresentative small sample.

That presents a problem in researching the market for a particular product. The producer may have chosen his target market precisely because it is unrepresentative. In a recent case a shop selling lingerie has no interest in national statistics about how much women spend on lingerie. It is not selling to the entire nation. It is selling only to those women who are extremely rich, self-indulgent, and live in Cheltenham. Or to their lovers. A most unrepresentative sample of the national population.

There are not many examples where very large collections of data over long time series are available in management. One of the few available data hoards is the collection of share price and stock market data, which provides such a happy hunting ground for finance researchers.

Much of the statistical analysis to be found in student management research projects is based on data derived from questionnaires. In order to make predictions about the behaviour, such as the buying behaviour, of a large population of target customers a questionnaire is sent to a smaller sample carefully selected to be representative of the larger population. The analysis of the responses from the small sample is used to draw inferences about the larger population. Since the questionnaire is widely used by student researchers and is dangerously unreliable in unskilled hands it merits a section to itself.

QUESTIONNAIRES

An eminent market researcher insists that questionnaires should be brought within the scope of the law relating to Dangerous Weapons. They have in his estimation caused more damage, loss of livelihood, and pecuniary damage than the molotov cocktail and the shillelagh combined.

Questionnaires are among the most widely used of all research methods to be found in student dissertations. They have several attractions. First, they are cheap and easy to administer. A number of questions are dispatched either by post or by interview to a selected sample of the population. Some of the recipients reply to the questions. Their replies are analysed.

Secondly, there is little difficulty of access. Provided that people reply to the questionnaires, the problem of access to data is solved. Contrast that with case study research where the researcher may have to negotiate long and hard to be allowed into the company, to talk to people, to see sensitive documents, attend confidential meetings where outsiders are not normally admitted.

Thirdly, there is less obvious likelihood of the researcher's presence influencing the replies or the behaviour of the people studied in questionnaires than there is, for example, in action research. Action research comes very close to consultancy. The researcher is working with the company to help it solve its problem and is, at the same time, studying the problem and the company's behaviour. Action research of this type raises the legitimate question: How can you say that you are observing the company's behaviour when you are also advising them what to do?

Questionnaire-based research avoids many of these difficult issues. Questionnaires are relatively cheap and easy to administer. Questionnaires allow relatively easy access to data but only to data which is easily accessible. Questionnaire data is often argued to be reasonably objective in the sense that the data collection methods can be carefully constructed to avoid the researcher influencing the answers, though the reverse can also be true.

Questionnaires do present their own inherent problems. Given the regularity with which student researchers use questionnaires, at least for their first research project, it is as well to know in advance what the problems are and how they can be overcome. A poorly designed piece of questionnaire research can invalidate the whole project.

The first problem is to design the questionnaire. The researcher should resist the temptation to invent his or her own questions. That imposes the researchers' concepts on the respondents. The aim is to discover the potential customers' thinking, not their reaction to questions about the researchers' thinking. One useful way to get a feel for what may be the right questions is to talk to potential customers about the product and listen to their comments. Observe what concepts, constructs, associations they attach to the product. This requires practice in the art of being a good listener. A good listener encourages customers to talk about the product without steering them or leading their responses. Some advertising and marketing agencies will hire a group of housewives for a small fee for an afternoon to talk in an unstructured way about a chosen product. Experience with these groups, sometimes grandly titled Qualitative Market Research Groups, leads to a certain scepticism. Scepticism is reinforced if one listens to the individuals talking afterwards about their experience of being part of the group. No doubt in the best of all possible agencies this technique can be controlled to yield valuable insights. In the less perfect cases the researchers are not hearing the constructs and concepts of potential customers. They may be hearing bored individuals, paid twenty-five pounds to talk about a product they know nothing about to a group of a dozen complete strangers, some of whom they have taken an instant dislike to.

The questionnaire should allow the target customers to express freely what they really feel about the product. Giving them a blank sheet of paper on which to write their thoughts might produce no response or responses so different that no generalizable conclusions could be drawn. So the questionnaire has to pose some specific unambiguous questions. The questions must relate to what the researcher wants to know and what the customer most wants to say about the product. This implies that both researcher and target customer should have an input into the design and choice of questions to be used. Talking and listening to real target customers will help identify the important issues and questions. Test running the questionnaire will help to debug it. Customers have a truly wonderous ability to misunderstand a question given the slightest chance.

The second problem in questionnaire design is to find foolproof questions. What the researchers had in mind when writing the question may not necessarily be precisely what comes into the respondent's mind on reading the question. The reader's reaction may be unexpected. A public company, which wished to be sensitive to what its staff felt about the company and whether they were content, employed a firm to ask the staff. The company thought that its staff might not feel free to talk uninhibitedly to their own bosses. So they employed an outside firm who used mail questionnaires which could be answered anonymously.

The questionnaires caused widespread offence. The feeling was summed up by one anonymous respondent who wrote across his questionnaire: 'If you want to know how I feel, talk to me. Don't employ strangers to talk to me for you.'

There was even a rumour that the questionnaire survey was a prelude to job cuts and redundancies. The questionnaires were either part of the softening up process or a sneaky way of identifying the disaffected and disgruntled.

The remedy is to prepare the questionnaire with great care. Then test it on colleagues. Then test it on a small sample of the target market. Be prepared to revise it at every stage. The creative imagination which complete strangers will willingly put into misunderstanding a questionnaire has to be seen to be believed.

The third problem with questionnaires is getting people to answer them. Most people in advanced countries receive their own weight in junk mail every week. Most of it goes straight into the trash can without being read. Junk mail that demands the recipients' time and attention to fill in a questionnaire has little chance of success. There needs to be some incentive to the recipient to give up the time and effort needed to respond. Some marketing organizations such as Reader's Digest offer the promise of a chance to win prizes in return for completed questionnaires. Appealing to some shared affiliation usually improves response rates. Professional accountants and lawyers tend to respond to questionnaires from their own professional institutes. A researcher who can tag on to such affiliations gets a better response rate. A good covering letter can help to win sympathy.

Even so response rates to questionnaires are often below 10%. That is a problem when the whole point of the sample is that it should be representative. When 90% of the target sample ignore the questionnaire, the 10% who do respond are by definition unrepresentative.

The fourth problem is getting anything meaningful out of a questionnaire. What questions from a complete stranger would you answer in writing? Presumably nothing of a confidential or revealing nature. Certainly nothing that could be used in evidence against you. Remember you do not really know who is asking the questions or why they want to know. Nor do you really know what they will do with your information once they have it. Is this the Infernal Revenue Service in disguise?

The fifth problem with questionnaires is making sense of the responses. Ninety per cent (perhaps) have not responded. Now the task is to draw representative information from the unrepresentative 10% who did reply. A few have spoiled their papers. Sometimes strange messages and pictures come back in response to a mailshot questionnaire. They do not help with the market research but they do raise the question of whether there is intelligent life on earth. The valiant 10% are further reduced by those who have misunderstood the question. From the remainder inferences have to be drawn which may affect other people's livelihoods, other companies' profits and investments.

The inevitable conclusion would seem to be: take great care in design and handling of questionnaire research but do not rely on it as your sole source of data. Find other means of testing and corroborating data. An example of this was the automobile designer who used a questionnaire, distributed via dealers, to discover vehicle purchasers' preferences for fittings and accessories on cars. The questionnaire research was simply one set of data among many which contributed to the manufacturer's thinking about car design. Competing manufacturers' cars were purchased and thoroughly analysed. Dealers were extensively consulted, as were trade journal editors, consumer associations, fleet managers and anyone else with relevant opinions. Experience from other countries was gathered. Prototypes were tested. Even so, it is still possible to get it wrong. Products still flop. But the better informed the company is, from a wide variety of carefully researched sources, the less likely it is to flop. Or so one hopes.

Useful guidelines for the design and use of questionnaires are provided by Easterby-Smith and colleagues.

Make sure that the question is clear.

Avoid any jargon or specialist language.

Avoid 'personal' questions.

Don't ask two questions in one item.

Avoid 'leading' questions which suggest indirectly what the right answer might be.

Provide a short covering letter explaining the purpose of the research and why/how the respondent was selected.

Start the questionnaire with brief instructions about how to complete it.

Vary the type of question occasionally, but keep similar types of questions together in bunches.

Start with simpler factual questions, moving on later to items of opinion or values.

Pilot the questionnaire on a small number of people before using it for real. This enables one to check that the items are easily understood and that there are no obvious problems to do with length, sequencing of questions, sensitive items, etc.

It is also important at this stage to see whether it is possible to analyse the data produced by the questionnaire . . . and whether the results appear to make any sense.

(Easterby-Smith et al., 1991)

A questionnaire survey which succeeds in all its aims and regularly obtains a 98% or better response rate is the National Census. National censuses are carried out in many countries. In Britain the Census takes place every ten years. The Census is so successful in achieving its aims that it is intriguing to inquire into its success.

The problem of designing the questionnaire is reduced in a number of ways. The Census has been carried out many times, so there is ample accumulated experience. Only simple factual questions like 'What is your name?' are asked. The researchers have less need to worry about people misunderstanding the question. Answering the questions is compulsory by law, which means that even if people do not like the design of the questionnaire they have no choice but to comply.

Foolproof questions are easier to devise because no opinions are sought. Only simple objective facts: 'What is your name?'; 'What is your address?'

Even so, some of these simple factual questions are value-laden. In trying to ensure that they avoid double counting people who move around, the pollsters choose one night of the year as their Census point. It is not precise enough simply to ask 'What was your address in 1995?' Some people may have changed address during that year. Some several times. The pollsters have to pinpoint one precise moment in time, such as 1 June. They choose the night of 1 June rather than the day because people move around more in the day than at night. So the question becomes: 'Where did you spend the night of 1 June 1995?'

Some respondents see more in that question than was intended. There is a suspicion that a percentage of the respondents do not answer that question with absolute truth.

The Census also carries questions about racial origins. This risks causing offence and suspicion about the purpose for asking the question.

Getting people to answer the Census questions is not a problem. The law demands it. Fierce penalties, including jail sentences, are threatened for anyone who does not answer. So fierce are the threats written upon the UK Census Questionnaire that many respondents find them offensive; but they still have to answer the questions.

Unwillingness to answer questions is thus overcome. In any case the questions generally avoid confidential or sensitive topics as far as possible.

Response rates and representative samples, major problems for most questionnaire surveys, are not a problem for the Official Census. Everyone has to respond: a 100% response rate.

How reliable is questionnaire data?

A questionnaire survey can still provide useful data, provided that the researcher has borne in mind the caveats discussed above. The question

'HOW DO YOU KNOW?'

is bound to be asked by examining body and by client company, and also by supervisor and by researcher in readiness for these inquisitors. Where a questionnaire has been used the questionnaire should be included as an appendix to the written report in order to allow the examiners to check that questions are neither leading nor misleading. They are interested to see whether the questions provide a reliable instrument for getting at the information the researcher seeks to uncover.

The report should also reveal details of the sample size, the way the sample was chosen, the response rate, the responses in detail to each question, the method of analysis of the data, and the conclusions drawn. The bulk of the data can usually be stored in the appendix, with the most powerful points summarized in the main body of the report. The inquisitors wish to test whether the data is sufficient to support the conclusions.

The researcher would be well advised to subject the project report to the most searching criticism before it is presented. Put yourself in the role of being the most perceptive, searching, suspicious examiner imaginable. What questions would such an inquisitor ask? How well does the project honestly stand up to the questioning? The aim here is not to bluff and bluster to shore up a defective case. The aim is for the researcher to discover where the weaknesses are in his or her own project as a prelude to finding more data to prove or disprove the existing conclusions. Weak areas in the project may point to a need for further inquiry. Further inquiry may show that the tentative conclusions should be jettisoned and replaced by better, more trustworthy, conclusions. It is better that the researcher should make that discovery rather than leave it to the examining panel. Having played the role of examiner to his or her own dissertation, the researcher should invite a colleague to play the role of examiner. No holds barred. No punches pulled. This is an examination designed to find the flaws while there is still time to do something to remedy them.

As a final practice the research supervisor is invited to take on the role of examiner. The supervisor knows the subject area, has seen many research projects, is a skilled and perceptive questioner. This should be the most searching and testing examination of the project research and findings that the supervisor can make it. It may well prove to be a more testing examination than the real examination by the panel. The supervisor has inside information. The practice examination is intended to find ways of improving the research, destruction testing it until there is no weak point left for the examining panel to find. The real examination panel has to decide pass or fail. The panel may decide to award a pass even where the research is not perfect.

The following questions may help the researcher to interrogate his or her own research.

- The research findings are mainly based on questionnaire data. What other evidence do you have?
- How do you know that your conclusions about the total population are valid? You have not asked the total population. You have surveyed only a much smaller number.
- How did you select your sample? Why do you believe it is representative?
- What is the downside risk if we follow your recommendations and they prove to be inaccurate?
- Tell me simply: What was the question you set out to answer? What is your conclusion in answer to that question?
- What is your evidence to support that conclusion?
- Let me stop you there. I am not asking for a detailed diary of everything you did during your research. The question put bluntly is: Why should I believe the conclusion? I do not doubt that you believe it. You have done the research and seen the evidence. I have not. Give me the evidence. Briefly. Simply. In your own words.
- What is it that you think you have done? [*This was a question which the examiners asked me on my PhD. It led to some very searching questioning.*]
- Is it reasonable to assume that the respondents are representative of the total population of interest to us? The sample is only a small proportion of the total population and the respondents are only a small proportion of the sample.
- Why did you choose these particular questions?
- In your own best estimate, what is the probability that if we implement your recommendations we shall earn the returns which you have estimated?
- What could go wrong? What is the worst that could go wrong, given bad luck, Murphy's Law, etc.?
- Provided we had the time and money to do the extra research, what else could we do to check out further the evidence and conclusions?
- As with any research you learn in the process of doing it. With the benefit of hindsight you can always see ways you could have done things differently, perhaps better. If you were doing this research again how would you improve on it? [*This is a question to think about before the real examination. You should also think about how much of the answer you want to share with the examiners.*]

Each of these questions is likely to lead to further questioning. Examining panels do not usually settle for the first answer they are given. It may well have been prepared in advance. The panel will want to probe and test. Once they pick up a scent of uncertainty they follow it up to see if it leads to weakness. Bluff and bluster is always the wrong tactic to use. A panel of examiners is on to it in a flash. Bluff and bluster marks the site of maximum uncertainty. Tell it like it is. Do not try to fool them. If the real examiners do not ask questions about a weak area there is no obligation to lead them there, but if they do light on an area where the data is only suggestive of a conclusion without being entirely conclusive, there is no point in trying to claim that the evidence is stronger than it really is. Remember that examiners are assessing the candidate's judgement. An apparent inability to distinguish weak evidence from strong can only cost marks. This is especially important for the part-time MBA student working on an in-house project. If a manager is seen to be hiding weaknesses in the evidence in order to win support for his or her preferred conclusion, colleagues may be very wary of ever trusting his or her judgement in matters of consequence.

A multi-method approach

6

We have seen from the foregoing that hypothesis testing experimental research can seldom be used in an absolutely pure form in management research. We have observed that statistical surveys and questionnaires are unlikely to be totally conclusive by themselves, though if skilfully employed they may yield valuable information. So how should we proceed? We still have a research project to do.

As is so often the case in management: when all else fails, try using common sense, and a range of techniques, none of which may be perfectly conclusive in themselves, but which between them may provide a greater deal of illumination.

AN EXAMPLE

Our task is to assess whether money which a company invests in management development is money well spent.

At this point the reader has enough knowledge to be able to tackle this research project. Jot down, if you will, on a piece of paper how you would go about tackling this research question. **DO NOT READ THE NEXT SECTION** until you have a project plan that satisfies you. The more thoroughly you complete this exercise, the more value you will gain from this book. The reason is that this exercise changes you from a passive reader to an active participant.

The project plan in Chapter 1 will provide a valuable guide.

SOLUTION: RESEARCHING MANAGEMENT DEVELOPMENT

1. DEFINE THE QUESTION

As always with a new research project, one begins by establishing what the question really is. What is the problem? What do we really want to know? Can we express the research as one focal question? In practice this usually takes time, thought, and conversation.

What is it that we want to know? An initial hypothesis

'Management development is a good thing'

or

'Management development is a worthwhile investment'

is not testable. Before we can measure a 'good thing' or a 'worthwhile investment' we would have to define in measurable terms what we mean by a 'good thing' or a 'worthwhile investment'.

The hypothesis might be refined as:

'Continuous investment in management development is associated with higher than average corporate profitability'

This second attempt at defining a testable hypothesis has some improvements. The outcome 'higher than average corporate profitability' is measurable. We can measure the companies' profits and compare them with the average for their industries. That should provide us with one set of data, in effect the dependent variable, which is reasonably clear, unambiguous and measurable. Specifying the independent variable as **continuous** investment in management development gets around the problem of time lags. We do not know whether the investment has immediate effect, or whether the effect takes years to become apparent, or whether it is the cumulative effect of sustained investment which is important. Thus we cannot simply move the investment up and down several times to see if there is an immediate movement up and down in profitability. It is unlikely that there would be an immediate response, but that would not prove that management development had no effect on profitability. The company would not be happy if we did succeed in moving its profitability down several times for the purposes of our experiment.

Notice that if we did discover evidence in support of our hypothesis we should not have established the direction of causality. If there were evidence that continued investment in management development was associated with higher than average corporate profitability we still would not know which was the cause and which the resultant effect. Was management development the cause (or a cause) of higher profitability? Or was it simply the case that only the more profitable companies could afford to spend money on management development?

What do we actually want to know? If we are researching into the effectiveness of management development we should presumably be interested to discover how best to do it. What are the most effective means of investing in management development, if any? Which approaches earn the best results? What are the mistakes and pitfalls to avoid? We are not just doing the research for idle curiosity. If we discover something useful we, or our clients, or the wider business community will want to profit from it. We may also want to use our discoveries to evaluate our clients' current practice to see whether and where there is opportunity for improvement.

2. IDENTIFY THE INFORMATION WE NEED

Where do we obtain the information that will allow us to make a judgement on the return on investment in management development? Clearly there are many sources of information, requiring different techniques of getting at the information. Between them they should throw a lot of light on the subject which interests us.

We are not the only people ever to be interested in this subject. In all probability people have thought, researched, and published material relevant to our inquiry. A good library will help us track down what is published. There will also be a great deal that practitioners know which is not yet published. Eventually we shall have to venture out of the library to go and talk to the expert practitioners, but not until we have read the published material. Expert time is rare and not to be wasted on material which we could have read in books and journals.

While still in the library we need to acquire a good grasp of the theoretical understanding of the subject. We know that we cannot measure the effectiveness of investment in management development in terms of a short-term ROI (return of investment) measure along the lines of £x invested yields a return of y% per annum. The correlation is not as direct, or as simple, or as immediate as that. And yet there must be some effect and some way of measuring it. If not, then we do not wish to waste the money. In these straitened economic times investment in acts of faith are best left to religious organizations. If the relationship between management development and corporate profitability is not direct, immediate, simple and straightforward, what do we think the relationship is, or may be? Is it, for example, that the firm has a strategic competence, a competitive advantage, that enables it to succeed against its competitors? And are we hypothesizing that management development is connected to that strategic competence? In short, what is the model, what is the theoretical basis that underlies our research? The literature on the subject is likely to offer us a range of models and theoretical frameworks which can help us to clarify our thinking before we plunge into the data gathering.

A word of caution here. The relationship between theory and data itself needs thinking about. You have to have some theory, some idea about what you are doing, before you can collect any data. Otherwise you would not know what data to collect. All observations would be equally relevant. But your pre-selected theory in selecting which data is relevant also ensures that you collect only data which fits the theory. The great danger here is that the data and the theory become mutually reinforcing. They may be wrong, but mutually reinforcing. Anyone who has ever enjoyed a heated argument with a devout communist or a religious fanatic of whatever religion will know how everything can be seen as proof positive of the fanatic's world view. The way of handling this problem is, first, to be aware of the several theories and models available to help explain the relationships between phenomena. Most especially is it important to be conscious of one's own models, theories, and assumptions concerning the subject. Nothing is more distorting of one's perception than the blinkers which one did not know one was wearing. Secondly, it is important to seek for data which disproves one's existing theory as ardently as one seeks for data which is deemed relevant within the theory.

Now we can venture out of the library and go and talk to people. There are many experts in the field who have valuable insights, experiences, theories, relevant to our inquiry. Not all of their information will be objective and unbiased. They have their own pet theories, prejudices, or recipes to sell. Here as everywhere our own judgement and discrimination is essential. It is important, too, to step outside of ourselves – to take a helicopter view, as it were, of our own implicit theory and prejudices. We are exercising our own judgement of what we are hearing. What is the basis of that judgement? We are all prisoners of our models, as the wise Tony Berry of Manchester Business School once remarked. To which one of his colleagues replied dreamily, 'I wouldn't mind being a prisoner of a model.' This, too, is an illustration of how our own preoccupations can cause us to interpret selectively what we hear.

Current best practice in companies will be of great interest to us. Some of the best managed companies invest heavily in management development. Why do they do it? How do they do it? What do they think they get out of it? What evidence do they have that they gain anything from it? Presumably the HR professionals in these high-spending companies have to justify their budgets and investments to their colleagues from other disciplines and to non-believers. What evidence do they give? This is, of course, not necessarily value-free data. It may be data selected to prove a point, to justify spending.

People have been on management development courses. What do they think? Here the interview and questionnaire techniques reviewed earlier can help us to ferret out the data.

Other people have researched what people gain, if anything, from courses. Various studies have tested managers before and after courses. Follow-up studies have tested them long after to see if there are lasting effects. Some such studies have used control groups to help isolate changes due to the course. Yet more studies have compared effectiveness of different courses, different learning methods, different teaching methods. All this vast mound of information is available via libraries, publications, and from the researchers themselves. So is follow-up information on what they did as a result of all their findings.

3. MAKE SENSE OF THE DATA GATHERED

From the many sources available our researchers can garner a vast amount of relevant information. Then the problem becomes not a lack of information but the need to make sense of it all, to distill what is relevant, and to draw worthwhile conclusions and recommendations. That is precisely why the time plan emphasized the need to give at least as much time, thought, and creative imagination to make sense of the data, to develop conclusions and recommendations and communicate them convincingly as is given to gathering the data.

The familiar pattern of the research project recurs here.

1. Identify the question to be answered

To do this it may be helpful to consider supporting questions, e.g. Who is the client? What do they want? What are their objectives? What is the precise question that this research is designed to answer? What is the desired end output; the deliverables?

2. Identify the information needed in order to answer the research question

To help with this task, use the supporting questions, e.g. What information do we need? Where is it located? How do you obtain it? Who has the information? How do you cross-check the reliability of the information obtained?

3. Make sense of the data gathered

Supporting questions that help in this task include, for example what published theories and insights attempt to make sense of this problem area (i.e. desk research)?
- How do practitioners see the situation? How do they make sense of the problem area? What models and insights do they use to work in this area (i.e. field research)?
- How do we pull together all of our data to make it meaningful to us and to our audiences?

- What does it all mean?
- We have a great mound of data gathered at great expense. What do we learn from it?
- How do we know?

The search for reliable knowledge

7

Let us review our progress thus far. We begin by choosing a subject for our research. The subject must be well chosen to serve several client groups: the scientific community through the advancement of knowledge; a corporate client who has a problem to be solved; corporate clients generally who may be able to apply our work to their own situations; and ourselves, learning by doing the research, and solving the problem.

The **project idea** is refined into a workable, manageable research project, achievable in the time and resources available. The chief technique to help us do this is the **project plan**.

The project plan is agreed with our several audiences before we set out on the research. We need to be sure before we begin that what we propose to do will satisfy our several audiences and consequently earn the several rewards which we seek. We seek to satisfy the academic examiners for the award of the degree; to satisfy the corporate client for the award of the fee; to satisfy our own need for meaningful, worthwhile experience, learning, and personal development. A good project enriches the researcher and each of the several audiences.

The aim of the project is to tell our audiences something which they did not already know. We take scrupulous care to ensure that what we tell them is reliable knowledge, distinguishing truth from falsehood.

When our recommendations are accepted, our clients will act upon them. We must be careful that we are not leading them astray. Through the project we are improving our own ability to distinguish truth from falsehood, and create new knowledge.

How then do we distinguish truth from falsehood? How will we recognize truth when we see it? The question has powerful practical relevance in management, as a few examples will show. In Britain there is a fierce debate around the closure of coal mines. One side states as its truth that British coal mines are uneconomical and must therefore be closed. The opposing side replies that this cannot be true. It cannot be true that it is more economical for Britain to leave its own coal in the ground, putting its miners out of work, and import coal from overseas. Both sides produce volumes of argument and numbers to prove their own case. Where is the truth?

In France fierce argument rages over the extension of the TGV route, the super-fast rail link from north to south in France. Those for the line argue that it will bring prosperity, improve the French infrastructure, and hence improve the French economy. Those against argue that it will destroy communities, existing prosperity, centuries of tradition, for the doubtful benefit of getting Parisians to the south one hour sooner. The sums of money involved are vast. The lives and livelihoods at stake are many. Where is the truth in all this? How does one search out the truth?

A British construction company is planning its strategy. One half of the Board argue for a radical programme to develop a major presence in the European market and the competitive capability to serve it to advantage. The opposition argue that we have a long history of losing money on foreign ventures. It is better to concentrate our efforts on the market where we have always done well and where we are traditionally the strongest player. Where does the truth lie? How can we establish what the truth is?

Some of the classics of management literature tell us how to manage our companies. Peters and Waterman in their book *In Search of Excellence* tell us why excellent companies are excellent and how we can learn from them to be excellent too. Michael Porter tells us how all companies should create their competitive strategies using his Industry Analysis and Generic Strategies. Geert Hofstede tells us how to understand foreigners and how to trade successfully with them.

Is any of this true? How do we know? How do we distinguish reliable, useful, helpful truth from misleading, dangerous, expensive, destructive falsehood?

The same problem has exercised researchers in the physical sciences the world over for centuries. The dominant method for distinguishing truth from falsehood has traditionally been **logical positivism**. The label 'logical positivism' has only been widely used recently when we have begun to realize that there may be other methods of arriving at a true test of knowledge. For a long time logical positivism has held such a dominant position in scientific thought that it seemed to be the only **scientific truth test**. It is the philosophy of logical positivism on which the experimental method, hypothesis testing, and statistical analysis are based. Through these techniques logical positivism still exerts a powerful influence on scientific thinking – which may include the thinking of your external examiner.

Science, as seen from a logical positivist standpoint, is concerned with discovering the fundamental laws of the physical world. It must be based on observable facts, nothing else. A fundamental law must hold good whenever and wherever it is observed, regardless of who observes it. Such a law is the Law of Gravity. Here we have a fundamental law of nature, testable a million times over, always with the same result; a truth quite independent of the observer or the whims of man or fashion.

Sadly the logical positivist test of truth, useful though it is, does not always solve all of our problems. There are times when we do not only want to understand external, objective, physical facts. Sometimes we want to understand people's emotions, behaviour, their ideas, likes and dislikes. Here we have moved away from the purely objective physical fact into the area of subjective ideas. Logical positivism was not designed to cope in this territory.

Sometimes the facts do not speak for themselves. We have to supply a theory to explain them. Where does the theory come from? Not from the objective, physical facts. The theory has to be supplied by the researcher.

These issues are central to discussions of what constitutes reliable knowledge. These are the issues and tests which will be applied to your research to discover whether what you say can be relied upon.

The key issues are:

- The scientific truth test
- Objectivity versus subjectivity
- The interplay of theory and data.

THE SCIENTIFIC TRUTH TEST

Thus far we have been exploring research methods which originated in the physical sciences. We have considered how these methods can be adapted for discovery in the social sciences, particularly in management. Underlying these models from the physical sciences is an implied philosophy, an idealized model of what constitutes scientific research. This idealized model is an attempt by many researchers in the physical sciences to answer for themselves the question:

How do you know?

You know that something is a fact, a valid piece of knowledge, if certain conditions are met. What are those conditions? Can we identify conditions, which are generally valid, that we can apply to each new discovery and each new theory, to everything in fact which purports to be knowledge to test whether or not it is true? The search was on for a litmus test which could distinguish clearly between truth and falsehood, between reality and illusion. The search has been pursued with as great an urgency as the quest for the Holy Grail, and for the Philosopher's Stone, both of which it resembles in some respects. Views and beliefs on the true test of valid knowledge have changed and developed continuously, accompanied by heated disputes. A history of the search for definition of the essential characteristics of real knowledge, for a reliable answer to the question 'How do you know?' is in effect a history of the development of humanity.

For the researcher presenting his or her findings to an audience it is helpful to know what the main issues and standpoints are concerning validity of knowledge. One examiner may take a standpoint that if knowledge is to be valid it must be objective. The examiner may choose to question the research from that objective standpoint. A second member of the examining panel may adopt a complementary view that subjective knowledge may be equally valid within certain circumstances and question the researcher from that viewpoint. Both examiners would reasonably expect the candidate for a higher degree to be conversant with both approaches and to have used both to test the research in progress. Objectivity and subjectivity are two alternative ways of considering validity in research. Must knowledge be entirely 'out there' independent of the researcher? Or can people's subjective interpretations, feelings, understandings be valid knowledge in themselves? Both viewpoints are arguable and frequently enthusiastically argued. Is reproducibility an essential requirement of true knowledge? That is, must it be possible for the same experiment to be repeated by some other researcher independently with the same results? Can that reproducibility test be applied realistically to management research where jobs, lives, and profits rather than inanimate variables are at stake? What is the relationship between theory and data? Should the researcher be innocent of all preconceived ideas allowing the data to speak for itself? Or is that a nonsense since all data is equally meaningless until someone attaches meaning to some of it? These are issues that should concern the researcher during the design and during the progress of the research. These issues are likely to interest the examiners. The researcher in the final phase of the research presents his or her findings and conclusions. He or she wants them to be accepted and acted upon. The examiners, both academic and corporate, are not going to accept and act upon anything until they have reliable answers to their key questions:

- **How do you know?**

the answer to which answers the related questions:

- **Do you know what you are doing?**
- **Are you a reliable adviser?**
- **Are the evidence, conclusion and recommendations reliable?**

The issues are important enough to merit contemplation.

OBJECTIVITY VERSUS SUBJECTIVITY

In the Vienna hospital case deaths decreased in the test ward when the medical professors did not attend autopsy before attending maternity ward. The drop in mortality rates was an objective fact, measurable, verifiable by independent observers. It did not depend on any subjective interpretations by researchers, patients, or inquisitive onlookers. It was not simply that patients felt better. They lived or they died, an objective fact, attestable by independent witnesses.

Thus one is tempted to conclude that knowledge which is objective, measurable, verifiable by independent observers is reliable, i.e. valid knowledge.

Some theoreticians have been tempted by this to argue that **only** knowledge which is objective, measurable, verifiable by independent observers is valid knowledge. If it is not objective, measurable, independently verifiable, it is not valid knowledge.

That strict rule makes it impossible to acquire knowledge about large areas of human experience. The way people feel about their work or their company is not a valid area of inquiry under these rules unless a way can be found of measuring dissatisfaction objectively as, for example, when manifest in staff turnover rates.

The early development of the science of psychology was bedevilled by this insistence on only studying phenomena which were objectively verifiable in the belief that only such knowledge was scientific. Pavlovian psychology, as in the famous dog-conditioning experiment, was acceptable. The researcher rings a bell then feeds the dog. Eventually the dog learns to associate bell ringing with food and salivates at the sound of the bell. Both observations, bell ringing and dog salivating, are objectively verifiable. Anyone can see them. But by contrast what goes on inside the mind is not observable and therefore not researchable. By this rule, human emotions, love, happiness, how we understand the world we live in, all are rendered inadmissible questions. There are still schools of psychology which hold to the view that only objectively verifiable phenomena 'out there' are worthy of study. But much of modern psychology has developed by finding reliable means of studying what goes on in the minds of people, in the mind as opposed to 'out there', subjective as opposed to objective. Study of subjective events is dangerous. Objective external phenomena are relatively safe. We can see them. You can see them. A complete stranger walking into the room can see them. The Vienna patient is alive or dead. No question about it. Nothing subjective about that. The bell rings and the dog dribbles. Or does not. Objective, observable fact.

If in our inquisitiveness we would like to understand better how people live in the world, if we want to understand people's subjective reality, happiness, joy, anger, and suchlike internal experiences, then we need ways of inquiring which can also yield reliable evidence and conclusions. Much of the recent developments in research methods in the social sciences have been concerned with creating such methods for discovering valid knowledge about subjective experience. The results are discussed in the following chapter.

The debate between the two approaches has a long history of often heated skirmishing. The label **positivist** is often applied to the approach which concerns itself only with externally verifiable objective data. The label **idealist** is often applied to the school of research that prefers to inquire into subjective reality.

> Throughout history Western philosophers have struggled with the epistemological question of what makes knowledge possible. Positivist thinkers and scientists from Democritus to Auguste Comte and Bertrand Russell have vigorously argued that true knowledge of 'reality out there' can be attained only through mathematical logic, sense observation, and scientific experimentation. But the eighteenth-century German philosopher Immanuel Kant had already demonstrated how illusory that notion had been. Kant demolished the hope that through hard scientific knowledge we can know the world as it is 'in itself'. Reality, Kant said, is 'out there' all right, but we are doomed never to approach it directly. Everything that passes as knowledge is in reality a construction of the human mind. True knowledge of reality, therefore is impossible.
>
> Parallel to the endless debate between the positivist and idealist tradition in Western thought there is another hidden or esoteric philosophical tradition. Advocates of this 'perennial' or 'hermetic' philosophy have proposed that true knowledge of reality is possible but only through mystical practice. This can lead to the uplifting of human consciousness and awareness to higher and more profound levels of cognition.
>
> (Markides, 1990)

The view that reality was external, 'out there' and thus independent of a human observer was summarized by the nineteenth-century epistemologist Auguste Comte as

All good intellects have repeated since Bacon's time, that there can be no real knowledge except that which is based on observable facts.
(Markides, 1990)

Easterby-Smith and colleagues identify eight key principles of positivism as follows:

1. *Independence:* The observer is independent of what is being observed.
2. *Value-freedom:* The choice of what to study, and how to study it, can be determined by objective criteria rather than by human beliefs and interests.
3. *Causality:* The aim of social sciences should be to identify causal explanations and fundamental laws that explain regularities in human social behaviour.
4. *Hypothetico-deductive:* Science proceeds through a process of hypothesising fundamental laws and then deducing what kinds of observations will demonstrate the truth or falsity of these hypotheses.
5. *Operationalisation:* Concepts need to be operationalised in a way which enables facts to be measured quantitatively.
6. *Reductionism:* Problems as a whole are better understood if they are reduced into the simplest possible elements.
7. *Generalisation:* In order to be able to generalise about regularities in human and social behaviour it is necessary to select samples of sufficient size.
8. *Cross-sectional analysis:* Such regularities can most easily be identified by making comparisons of variations across samples.

It is worth repeating that these propositions are not simply the view of any single philosopher; they are a collection of points that have come to be associated with the positivist viewpoint.
(Easterby-Smith *et al.*, 1991)

These key characteristics of positivism were intended to help all inquirers after knowledge to ensure that what they thought was knowledge was in fact real and reliable, not illusory, or self-deception. And yet looking through Easterby-Smith's list it is interesting to observe how many of these characteristics are powerfully inappropriate to some areas of management research. For example, the criterion of independence would raise major questions about the kind of research where the researcher engages with the client company to help it to solve a problem. Much of action research is precisely of this kind. If one is going to engage in action research or participative research one has to look again at the question of independence. It is not an irrelevant question but the positivist formulation of the question is not entirely appropriate. The action researcher is affecting the organization which he or she seeks to observe, and must take that into account in making sense of the observations. Value-freedom is often an inapplicable criterion in management research in the sense in which Easterby-Smith *et al*. have defined it. More often the research subject has been identified precisely because people are strongly interested in it. It is a meaningful problem whose effective solution would be most interesting to them.

As the research proceeds the researchers can gain considerable value from testing their research against these tests of validity. The questions to ask of one's research are:

- Does the research stand up to these criteria?
- Are these criteria appropriate and relevant to this research? If not, why not?
- If these criteria do not apply, what criteria should stand in their place?
- How does the research stand up to these more appropriate criteria?

These questions are worth considering at the research design stage, while the research is in progress, in writing up the research, and in preparation for the examination. They also help to give a useful insight into the examiner's mind. These are the sort of questions acute examiners may well ask.

THE INTERPLAY OF THEORY AND DATA

The second major issue concerning the reliability of conclusions is a continuation of the first. Are the conclusions and recommendations wholly borne out by the facts? Or are they the result of the presenter's subjective interpretation of the facts?

In most business presentations the conclusions and recommendations depend on both, on a combination of factual evidence and the presenter's subjective interpretation of the evidence. This leads the audience into dangerous territory. It is the audience to whom will fall the responsibility of acting on the recommendations. The audience must decide whether to accept the recommendations and implement them or to reject them and take some other course of action. The audience has to form a judgement on three factors:

- the reliability of the evidence;
- the reliability of the presenter's interpretation: of the evidence and conclusions, and recommendations based on that interpretation;

- the reliability of the presenter in investigating the subject and in selecting which facts to present.

This is why it is so important for the presenter to avoid any temptation to overstate the case, or to make the evidence appear stronger than it is. If the audience find that the presenter has overstated one piece of evidence, they may well form an instant judgement that this is not a reliable witness or guide. Then the case is irretrievably lost, and with it the credibility of the presenter. The audience has to decide:

1. Do we reach the same conclusion based on these facts?

Equally important the audience has to decide:

2. Are these facts as presented to us an accurate and complete representation of the reality of the situation? Are we being told the whole story?

These questions are of greatest importance whether the researcher is presenting a recommendation for an individual company's strategy or a major new theory of management. In Case 1 the recommendation may be, for example, that the company should move into this new country in a particular way. Acceptance of the advice would mean major investment of capital, management time, deployment of people and resources, all of which could be profitably employed elsewhere. Does the evidence support the conclusion and justify the investment and effort? Is the evidence reliable? In Case 2 a theory is being proposed which, if accepted, would change the way we manage our organizations. Not just one company, but all companies that act on the new theory. Is it acceptable? Does the evidence justify the conclusion? Are we all sufficiently convinced to act upon it?

This interplay of facts and subjective collection and interpretation of facts is an essential part of any research. But it is also problematic. The researcher chooses which facts to collect, which observations to make. The facts do not usually speak for themselves. They have to be interpreted. The reliability of the interpretation and of the research on which it is based is in large measure a product of the reliability of the researcher. The researcher has to be continuously self-aware, on guard to observe the way in which he or she is selecting and interpreting the data, and why. As Reason and Rowan (1981) observe: 'Valid research rests above all on high quality awareness on the part of the co-researchers.'

Scientific methodology needs to be seen for what it truly is: a way of preventing me from deceiving myself in regard to my creatively

formed subjective hunches which have developed out of the relationship between me and my material.

(Rogers, 1981)

In management investigations the need is equally powerful for contin-
ual vigilance on the part of the investigators and the clients that evidence and interpretation are not biased towards some preferred outcome. Managers may well be investigating their own company; making
recommendations that will affect resources allocated to their own
department; presenting conclusions to people who are in the same
political hierarchy that they themselves depend on. Some managers
investigating a new business opportunity may be tempted to treat the
investigation rather as an exercise in competing for additional resources
akin to the annual budget struggle. The underlying questions in the
investigator's mind have become: 'How do we make a case for this?
How do we convince the Board to let us do this? And give us the
resources to do this?' That kind of bias does not lead to an objective
evaluation of what may be in the best interests of the organization as
a whole. For the new venture to work optimally requires that the
manager has the objectivity to evaluate impartially and critically what
is best for the organization as a whole, and the subjective commitment
to pursue it with energy. A manager investigating his or her own
company can be biased in perception without necessarily being concerned to feather his or her own nest. Working in a company for any
length of time, one sees ways in which it could be improved. An
energetic, committed manager may develop a powerful drive to change
the company to improve its performance. The task then is to convince
other people of the desirability of the change. The research project may
be seized upon as the ideal vehicle for promoting the change. Therein
lies one of the greatest dangers of the in-house project. The subjective
commitment to the proposed course of action may make it intensely
difficult to test it objectively and impartially. The self-discipline which
the manager must impose upon himself or herself requires that he or
she searches equally hard for evidence which disproves his or her pet
strategy. In most cases discovery of evidence which contradicts the pet
strategy leads the manager to a better strategy.

That powerful interplay of subjectivity and objectivity, of factual data
and personal interpretation of the data is common to all the social
sciences. Jung observes that in psychology one cannot progress far by
sitting in an armchair. One has to go out and look at the data, to
observe, and to experience. The moment one does that, one is interact-
ing with the observations and experience, working with them, striving
to make sense of them, seizing on some facts, casting others aside.

Although not a few people think that a psychology can be written *ex cathedra*, nowadays most of us are convinced that an objective psychology must be founded above all on observation and experience. This foundation would be ideal if only it were possible. The ideal and aim of science do not consist in giving the most exact possible description of the facts – science cannot compete as a recording instrument with the camera and the gramophone – but in establishing certain laws, which are merely abbreviated expressions of many diverse processes that are yet conceived to be somehow correlated. The aim goes beyond the purely empirical by means of the *concept*, which, though it may have general and proved validity, will always be a product of the subjective psychological constellation of the investigator. In the making of scientific theories and concepts many personal and accidental factors are involved. There is a personal equation that is psychological and not mere psychophysical. We see colours but not wavelengths. . . . The effect of the personal equation begins already in the act of observation. One sees what one can best see oneself. . . .

But the personal equation asserts itself even more in the presentation and communication of one's own observations, to say nothing of the interpretation and abstract exposition of the empirical material. Nowhere is the basic requirement so indispensable . . . that the observer should be adequate to his object, in the sense of being able to see not only subjectively but also objectively. The demand that he should see only objectively is quite out of the question, for it is impossible. We must be satisfied if he does not see too subjectively.

(Jung, 1971)

Harré takes up the argument that new knowledge requires both evidence and an observer to understand the evidence.

Most realists would argue that facts and theories are not independent. Facts are revealed to a human observer who uses a theory to identify significant items from the complex flux of experience. It follows that a realist can admit that there may be real indeterminateness in the world. The world may be made determinate to human experience by acts of observation and categorisation which impose structures and boundaries on the deliverances of sense. There are suggestions of this in sub-atomic physics, but the point is of central importance to the human sciences. . . . Many human actions may be indeterminate, deliberately left vague and so open to various interpretations.

(R. Harré, in Reason and Rowan, 1981)

This discussion should leave the researcher with a clearer idea of the problem to be managed. It may be summarized as follows. The facts are unlikely to speak for themselves. Someone, i.e. the researcher, has to interpret and make sense of the facts and draw conclusions and recommendations from them. The researcher does so on the basis of concepts and theories which the researcher supplies and which are not implicit in the data. Research is therefore an interplay of data and theory, of objective and subjective reality. The researcher, in observing the data and collecting evidence, is selective of which data to observe, which to collect. In selecting some data in preference to other data, the researcher is also imposing his or her own theory (or bias) on the situation. The quality and reliability of the resulting conclusions and recommendations are dependent as much on the quality and reliability of the researcher as of the data. The researcher needs to be continuously self-reflective and aware of his or her own biases, selectivity, and theories in selecting and interpreting the evidence. The audience needs to form their own judgement both on the reliability of the evidence and the reliability of the researcher. The researcher has to take scrupulous care to guard against misleading the client audience and against misleading the researcher him/herself. The client audience has to take scrupulous care to test that this is so.

No one can tell in advance if a move into a new market will be profitable or not. One can only weigh up the evidence, estimate the probability of success, and identify what seems to be the best way of proceeding to improve the chances of success. No one can say with certainty that this is the right way to create a strategy. One can only say that, on the basis of all the evidence presently available, this seems the most likely to work, until such time as we have something better.

Similarly, the researcher has to take scrupulous care to test his or her own data sources – even when the data comes from supposedly impeccable sources.

Frequently when researching a market you will have to rely on other people doing a lot of the work for you. Where good published statistics are available, use them, but use them with caution. Two current examples illustrate the opportunities and the dangers. One project examines the future prospects for a company producing steel tubes for the North Sea oil industry. The prospects for the company in the North Sea depend heavily on forecasts of future activity in the oil industry, proven reserves, rates of exploitation, etc. It would not be feasible for the researcher, Ken, to conduct a personal geological survey of the North Sea during the period of his project. Instead the necessary data is available from UKOIA, the UK Oil Industry Association. But before taking the data at face value, Ken has to test its reliability. Why was it prepared? Does UKOIA have an axe to grind?

Before relying on data and putting your name to it, quote your sources, test the reliability of the evidence and conclusions. When the data is important to your own research try to find two or more independent sources of data to corroborate or test the published conclusions.

Statistics are usually collected for a purpose. They are published for a purpose. This is particularly apparent in the case of national economic and unemployment statistics. A researcher, Ian, is investigating the prospects for the executive recruitment market in Germany. He needs to compare growth rates in the British and German economies and unemployment rates in the two countries. He has run into difficulties because such statistics are collected and published by institutions that have a strong vested interest in making the figures look good, namely government. The British government has changed the way it calculates the unemployment figures sixteen times recently. Whether this leads to a more accurate total or a rosier picture is open to question. Other national governments have their own preferred ways of calculating their own unemployment and economic statistics, and their own interests to serve. The task of recalculating all the relevant statistics of different countries to bring them back to a common basis for comparison would be a mammoth task beyond the scope and time available for Ian's project. Fortunately for him the task has been undertaken by OECD, the Organization for Economic Cooperation and Development, a relatively independent supranational body. Ian's report puts this rather well.

Lies, Damned Lies and Unemployment Statistics

There can be few other statistics which are collected at such great expense as unemployment data, only to be later 'corrected' in order to reflect the 'true' labour market situation. To allow for fair comparisons only OECD data are quoted here. The OECD tries to publish data cleansed of national fudge factors.

Before relying on data supplied by other people it is necessary to enquire carefully to discover what are the facts and what are the interpretations which they place on these facts. How reliable are the facts and the conclusions? How reliable are the people reporting the conclusions? In fact just the same questions that your readers will be asking of you.

THE SEARCH CONTINUES

We still need to distinguish reliable knowledge from nonsense. We still need to distinguish truth from falsehood.

The traditions of the physical sciences give us one set of tests in logical positivism. But they are not always relevant or useful in the areas we want to explore.

So what else is there?

We do not accept everything, every theory, every guru on blind faith. Too much is at stake. This is for real. People's lives, incomes, businesses, countries, economies are run and possibly ruined on the basis of what passes for management and economic knowledge and theory. We have to do our best to get it right.

What tests do we have? First and foremost those supplied by experience, common sense, and cunning. We are not babes in arms. We have survived so far and we have learned from the experience. We know that we have to be on our guard, to take nothing on trust untested. Often we have to take a risk on the best information we can get, knowing that the information is not perfect.

There are several tests we can use to probe facts, the theories, the conclusions before we place too much reliance on them, for example:

- *Generalizability:* Are the conclusions based on a wide enough range of cases and companies? Or is the theory totally irrelevant to all companies other than the one that the researchers happen to have studied? How generalizable is it?
- *Intersubjectivity:* This is the way I see it. Do other people see it this way, too? Or am I kidding myself?

I see a ghost walking down the stairs. If you see it, too, I will believe it is there. If you do not see it I will conclude that I am imagining it. Michael Porter believes that there are only two ways to compete: do it better or do it cheaper, labelled as 'differentiation' or 'cost leadership'. Does that match your experience? Do you believe in generic strategies? And ghosts?

- *Critical self-awareness:* Being perpetually on our guard to make sure we are not fooling ourselves.
- *Repetition:* Show me that again. If it worked once, will it work again? How much evidence do you have?
- *Verisimilitude:* Does the theory ring true? Do the recommendations strike you as credible? Try them on an audience and see if they believe them.
- *Theoretical congruence:* You are not the first person to think about this type of problem. What do the others have to say?

Each of these tests is worth exploring in more depth.

GENERALIZABILITY

Within the old paradigm of positivist methodology a fact was considered true if it was generalizable; that is, if it could be seen to be true in every case in which the law applied. Thus Newton's proposition of the Law of Gravity declared that all apples falling out of trees will always fall downwards. The observation was true not only of Newton's garden or of Granny Smith's. It applied to gardens in general and to apples in general. More than that it was found to apply to all solid objects which are heavier than air. It was generalizable.

Some areas of management research allow generalizable statements to be made. Where there are large populations of similar events research may discover relationships that apply generally to all such events. For example, share prices on the stock market are affected by corporate dividend policy. This can be tested many times for many shares of many companies in many countries over long periods of time and is found to apply generally, that is to all of them.

Some areas of management research do not readily suit the generalizability test, notably where populations are small – where, for example, we may be investigating what happens in one particular company. Then the focus of our interest may be how to manage this company at this particular difficult time. We may be less interested in general truths about all companies ever more. Having learned how to manage this one company can we say that we now know something about managing companies generally? Does what we have learned in this company apply to other companies? Is it generally valid? How do we know?

The question is of interest to managers whose ability to manage is based largely on experience gained in a small number of companies. Does the experience gained in managing three or four companies qualify a person to manage other companies?

Much management research is based on in-depth study over a long period of time in one or a few companies. The small sample is necessitated because the researchers are not studying a few simple variables but rather a large complex system. To understand, for example, the way that a company manages the transformation from leadership by a single owner-driver to the larger more systematized professionally run organization requires the study of many aspects of the company over a long period of time. To study one company in such depth may take years of research. A large sample of several hundred might take several centuries to complete and an army of researchers. But in the absence of a large sample, how can researchers be sure that the conclusions drawn from a study of one company (or three, or five) would be valid for other companies?

There are numerous examples of managers with successful experience in one company being engaged to run or advise another quite different company. So, Bob Horton, ex-chief of BP, is appointed chairman of British Rail. Sir John Harvey-Jones, ex-chairman of ICI, is given the task of advising on the management and strategy of the Morgan Motor

Company Ltd. There have been several examples of senior managers of commercial companies being recruited to head business schools. There have been no extensive studies as yet of how the transfer works. What evidence there is at present is largely anecdotal and contradictory. We simply do not know as yet whether a manager successful in one company is likely to be successful in another company, nor how to improve the chances of success. Is managerial success in one company generalizable to other companies? We simply do not know, though much recruitment is based on the hope that it will be.

If we are to learn from experience of companies, either from managing them ourselves, or from studying them in great depth, then we need a means of testing the validity of knowledge drawn from small samples.

The development of research methods capable of generating reliable knowledge concerning the management of complex organizations is still continuing. The older methods developed in the physical sciences can be adapted to cope with some social situations. In addition, other methods of acquiring knowledge, other tests of validity continue to be added. The following tests of validity are valuable.

INTERSUBJECTIVITY

In other words, it's less likely to be a figment of my imagination if other people can see it, too.

> So we have to learn to think dialectically, to view reality as a process, always emerging through a self-contradictory development, always becoming; reality is neither subject nor object, it is both, wholly independent of me and wholly dependent on me. This means that any notion of validity must concern itself both with the knower and with what is known: valid knowledge is a matter of relationship. And of course this validity may sometimes be enhanced if we can say we know, rather than simply I know: we move towards an *intersubjectively* valid knowledge which is beyond the limitations of one knower.
> (Reason and Rowan, 1981)

Intersubjectivity is an incomplete guard against self-deception. It leaves open the possibility that truth is a delusion shared. Additional tests are necessary.

CRITICAL SELF-AWARENESS

If our knowledge results from a blending of data and our personal interpretation of the data, then we need to be as aware of what we bring to the research situation as we are of the data. We should study the data and we should study our own capability and predilections as research instruments. We see this starkly when team teaching a case study or working in a consulting team in a company. Different members of the team see the problem differently. One might almost say that they see a different problem. And since they see the problem differently they see different possible solutions with different emphases:

> This kind of high quality awareness can only be maintained, and the problems of counter-transference managed, if the co-researchers engage in some form of personal and interpersonal maintenance and development. It seems to us that the researcher must actively explore the stirrings of his or her unconscious while engaged in research, and it is essential that she or he is practised and competent in a discipline for doing this. Our own preferred discipline is co-counselling. . . . But co-counselling is not the only answer; there are many disciplines to self-awareness. . . . We are simply repeating the ancient injunction *know thyself* which has been repeated (and repeatedly ignored) through the ages.
>
> (Reason and Rowan, 1981)

Cumberlidge (1978) puts the point succinctly:

> We can regard an inquiring process as being scientific to the extent that the researcher can identify the relationship between his inputs and his outputs.

Notice that this is very different from the positivist paradigm that the observer must be independent of what is researched, a fly on the wall having no effect on or relationship to what is being observed.

REPETITION

Learning, like research, may usefully be described as a cyclical process, or rather a spiral. The researchers have some notions about a subject, the beginnings of a theory. They collect data to test the theory. On the basis of reflecting on the data they create a new improved theory. Then they set out to test the new theory with fresh data. In the same way the experience of working in one company can provide us with the basis for a personal theory of how to manage, to the extent that we reflect on it. If we want to test its reliability then we need to test it in a new company in new circumstances.

> Two organisations researched in depth is presumably a sounder base for prediction than one. And three is a larger sample than two. But

our aim is not to reach so large a sample as to simulate randomness. We are not seeking to discover a pattern of variables across a large and random sample. The purpose of the second case study is to give us a better understanding of the first.

(Raimond, 1986)

VERISIMILITUDE

Does the theory ring true to the critical audience? Does it seem to fit in with the accumulated experience of colleagues working in similar areas? The new theory may not be the way they have been in the habit of thinking about the situation. It may even at first sight be earth shattering. But when they have recovered from the initial shock, does it seem to them worthy of consideration? Does it fit well with their experience even if it is a novel way of conceptualizing it?

In effect the researchers are using their colleagues' accumulated experience as a further test of the new theory. The experiences of those colleagues have passed through the minds of those colleagues. What is reported is not objective, untouched data. It arises out of the interaction of the experiences and 'the psychological constellation of the investigator', to borrow Jung's phrase. Colleagues are not testing the researchers' new theory against some touchstone of ultimate truth. They are testing it against the 'creatively formed subjective hunches which have developed out of the relationship between me and my material'. Testing one's theorizing on colleagues is a useful test but not wholly conclusive either way.

There is always a need in research for colleagues, peers, mentors, friends willing to act as enemies, who can challenge and shock one out of habitual ways of thinking and experiencing.

(Reason and Rowan, 1981)

THEORETICAL CONGRUENCE

We are probably not the first people ever to have thought about the particular problem that concerns us. Our conclusions, our theory follows in a line of other work in the same area. It should be tested against that existing body of theory. It may not agree with it. In all probability it will not agree with it in some particulars. But it cannot ignore it. Where the new theory departs from the old it must explain and justify the difference. Some elements of the new theory may also be supported by existing knowledge from related areas. This also needs to be explored for the additional insights it may offer. Part of the richness of management research is that it can draw on a rich heritage from many scientific disciplines.

IN CONCLUSION

The aim of this chapter has been to raise the researcher's awareness of the need to tackle the question

'How do you know?'

and of the issues involved and the methods available for answering it. It is one of the most important questions to be asked of any research. It is also one of the most telling questions in a *viva voce* examination when the research is presented to corporate client and to academic examiner.

Management research has drawn extensively on the research methods of the physical sciences, methods such as experimental testing of hypotheses, statistical analysis of large population samples in the search for correlations, causal relationships, and the immutable laws of nature. To use these research methods in the social sciences, and particularly in management, substantial adaptation has been necessary. In addition, management and the social sciences have developed their own methods of inquiry and, consequently, their own tests of validity of the knowledge gained. We shall examine the newer developments in management research technique, such as participative research, action research, and endogenous research in the following chapter. But first it has been our aim to sensitize the researcher to the major issues involved, since the quality of the research is largely dependent on the quality of awareness of the researcher.

New methods in management research

8

At first management researchers began by following the methods of the physical sciences, adapting them as necessary to cope with the problems of discovering and of creating new knowledge in the new science and art of management. Like any new subject, the current formulation of management began by borrowing from older traditions until it grew strong enough to shape its own. Much of our modern knowledge of management has a relatively short history. Modern management theorists usually trace the ancestry of their ideas only as far back as the writings on industrial management of the 1920s and 1930s. Even these writings have a curiosity value, seeming to describe a world long gone, like a Dickens' novel. Most current management knowledge, especially that taught in business schools, has been created within the most recent twenty years. The subject is developing and changing fast. What was considered best practice or generally accepted principles twenty years ago is rapidly being discarded and replaced. That makes management an exciting field to work in, a new science with rapidly moving frontiers. It also raises the question of whether much of management theory and practice is real knowledge and science or only a passing fashion. How do you know?

Some managers have taken to studying much older texts on management from earlier civilizations. A reprint of the Chinese treatise on *The Art of War* by Sun Tsu is presented by its publishers as the fastest selling book on management in the USA. Sun Tsu wrote it four thousand years ago. Musashi's *Book of Five Rings*, a Japanese treatise on strategy, war, and the ethical and military code of the warrior, is enjoying a new popularity centuries after it was written. Machiavelli's *The Prince* is often cited as an important textbook on management, though its theme was statecraft in renaissance Italy. Do these classics from earlier ages have relevance to our present attempts to learn how to manage better our modern organizations? How do we know? What tests can we apply to these old texts, theories, and practices to see if they have relevance to us now? Do they contain useful knowledge for us or for history?

Management does have fashions. Some techniques achieve a rapid popularity and soon fall from favour, enjoying a brief life-cycle like a consumer product. Management By Objectives was the in technique for a while. Before that Work Study with its associated paraphernalia of work measurement, time and motion studies, and piecework rates were ideas that every manager must have in order to be thought professional. Michael Porter's ideas on Generic Strategies and Industry Analysis have enjoyed a similar vogue at the end of the 1980s and the beginning of the 1990s. Will Porter's models pass out of favour to become a historical curiosity? Or will they prove to be of permanent value, a stepping stone from which further advances will be made? More generally, does management accumulate a permanent and growing body of knowledge so that the next generation is better equipped than its predecessor? Or is today's best practice simply whatever works today in today's circumstances, a product and a response to a temporary set of conditions? Do managers and researchers through their experience and reflection have the possibility of learning something of lasting worth? Or are management principles and current best practice as ephemeral as a fashion product, here today gone tomorrow? How do we know? How do we identify whether a management principle, practice or theory is real knowledge of lasting worth, and a step forward in our understanding? We have between us been running thousands of organizations for many years. Have we learned anything?

Management differs from the physical sciences in a number of ways that make it necessary to develop new techniques specifically suited to studying its peculiar phenomena. In management we are often studying people, not inanimate objects. We are studying the behaviour not of electrons, protons, and gases but our fellow human beings. That raises the question of what should be the proper relationship of the researcher to the people he or she is studying. Can one ethically do research **on** people? Or should it be **with** people? Should the people whose behaviour we are studying be fully in the picture about what is going on? Should they be informed and participating in the study? If they are, then the old requirement from positivism that the subject studied should not be influenced by the existence of the research situation is no longer tenable. It may be that an electron behaves in the same way whether a scientist is watching it or not. Not so an assembly line worker or a manager. They know they are being watched. They interpret the situation, make their own sense of it, manage the situation to suit themselves. So researchers have to find ways of working with people that allow both sets of participants to understand what is going on. That is not a possibility under the strictest application of the positivist-empiricist tradition of research. A different paradigm has to be invented.

There are ethical issues in the consideration of whether one does research *on* people or *with* people to which we in the late twentieth century are especially sensitive. The Mengele experiments on people in concentration camps during the 1939–45 period are not forgotten. During 1992 Channel 4 television in Britain showed film of an American experimental project to discover the long-term effects of syphilis if it was not treated. Patients with syphilis were studied over a period of twenty-five years without being given any curative treatment. They were not told that they were not being given any curative treatment. They were not told that the purpose of the experiment was to observe the effects on them of the untreated disease. During the television film different observers described this as 'a necessary experiment in the interests of science'; others described it as an 'atrocity'. These two words 'science' and 'atrocity' when brought together to describe one event have symbolized a major concern for our era.

The relationship between research and consultancy has caused much deep thought, particularly in the business schools and universities. What is the difference between research and consultancy? If I help a company to solve a problem is that consultancy? If by helping several companies to solve similar problems I learn from the experience, and consequently propose some new theory or technique, is that research? If it is not, then how does one do research in management which does not involve working with companies? Does it perhaps depend on my motive for being there? Perhaps one could consider a definition that says that if I am there purely to discover knowledge, then that is research. Whereas if I am there to work for the company and get paid for it, that is consultancy. That does not work as a definition because one can do both at the same time – help the company and learn from the experience. Indeed, one may go a stage further and help the *company* to learn from the experience. And to learn how to learn. Nor does it seem sensible to declare that 'It's only knowledge if you don't get paid for it.' From my own point of view one valid test of the value of a piece of research is whether anyone will pay for the outcome. If no one values it, it may not be valuable; a harsh test and one that is not always applicable. It must be possible to learn from consulting assignments. We are working in companies, on problems, investigating situations, developing solutions. We do not presumably want to rule out that whole wealth of experience as being somehow invalid. But if we do want to use experience of helping companies as a way of learning about them, we must develop a way of doing so which allows us to extract valid knowledge from the experience. To take a crude example, considering only those options which the paying client is known in advance to favour is not research. Nor is it good consultancy. The researcher must have independence of spirit and a willingness and freedom to consider all the options. But that is also likely to be true of high-quality consulting, as consultants would be quick to remind us. Perhaps we can say that research occurs when the study is set up and conducted in order to glean valid, generalizable knowledge, and that it is possible to be both researcher and consultant at the same time. Those two roles need not necessarily be mutually exclusive, though they will require careful management to satisfy both. Methodologies such as action research, participative research, endogenous research are ways of working as both consultant and researcher, contributing to the client and to the body of scientific knowledge simultaneously.

Much management research is conducted with small samples, with case studies of individual companies. Consequently we need research methodologies that allow us to gain reliable knowledge but which do not depend on large samples, huge populations, infinitely repeatable experiments or laboratory conditions.

As a result of these differences between the physical sciences and the social sciences, and most particularly management, there is a strong need for additional tools to help us to get to grips with what happens in the management of organizations. Methods of research developed in the physical sciences and social sciences give us a foundation on which to build. This has so far been supplemented with additional techniques such as action research and participative research. These additional techniques are explained in the following pages for two reasons. First, they add to the researcher's armoury of research methods. Secondly, they demonstrate that it is possible to break many of the old rules and yet still do good research and discover valid, useful new insights and understanding. These additional methodologies are by no means the complete answer in themselves. They are additions to the researcher's repertoire. The field of research methodology in management is still developing fast. A methodology is worthwhile if it allows you to generate reliable answers to the question:

How do you know?

ACTION RESEARCH

Action research is a collaboration between the researchers and the organization studied, which is also the client. The researchers are working in the company for two purposes: to help solve the client problem and to add to the stock of human knowledge. Clark describes the problems involved.

> Action Research has three task masters: the sponsor, the behavioural science practitioner, and the scientific community. The fact that these dissimilar groups are related for the duration of a project imposes many strains, and it must be observed that one of the major problems facing the action researcher is the devising of appropriate administrative mechanisms for simultaneously linking and separating these groups.
>
> Action Research is one strategy for influencing the stock of knowledge of the sponsoring enterprise. In that sense, it is a strategy for distributing knowledge, but the ideal project is one in which both the behavioural scientists and the sponsors benefit through having a better understanding of a particular problem. Typically the sponsors are concerned to ensure that they get 'value for money spent' and hence not always especially concerned with the theoretical activities and interests of practitioners.
>
> (Clark, 1979)

Because there is benefit to the company studied as well as to the scientific community, the company may the more readily grant access. Few companies will open themselves to strangers and researchers unless there are substantial benefits to themselves.

> Action Research is also concerned with adding to the stock of knowledge of scientists and is said to be a way of gaining privileged access to data and situations which are not normally accessible to basic researchers.
>
> (Clark, 1979)

The partnership between the consulting interests and the research interests are emphasized by Rapaport in a definition of action research.

> Action Research aims to contribute *both* to the practical concerns of people in an immediate problematic situation and to the goals of social science by joint collaboration within a mutually acceptable ethical framework. . . . Action Research is a type of applied social research differing from other varieties in the immediacy of the researcher's involvement in the action process.
>
> (Rapaport, 1970)

The researchers are not just studying the situation. They are changing it.

Action Research must possess an aspect of direct involvement in organisational change, and simultaneously it must provide an increase in knowledge.

(Clark, 1979)

In effect the researcher has become a player in the drama as well as being a spectator. Maintaining both roles is difficult but essential. The researcher has to maintain conscious awareness of both roles all the time. To slip entirely into one role to the detriment of its partner can only mean that one set of clients is dissatisfied. Either the researcher learns and increases his or her experience but fails to help the client organization with the problem, or the consultant solves the client's problem, learns little or nothing from it, fails to relate it to the existing body of scientific knowledge, and adds nothing to it. Then the scientific community is dissatisfied. By fulfilling only one set of client requirements and neglecting the other the research student ends up with either no degree or no fee. Satisfactory performance entails satisfying both client groups and winning both prizes.

Action Research is an approach to applied social research in which the action researcher and a client collaborate in the development of a diagnosis of and solution for a problem, whereby the ensuing findings will contribute to the stock of knowledge in a particular empirical domain. The emphasis tends to be upon the need to understand a total system in conducting such an analysis so that many action research projects are in fact special kinds of single case study, though there are examples of multiple case study projects. The whole gamut of research designs and approaches to data collection can be and have been deployed in action research . . . self-administered questionnaires, structured interviews, participant observation, unstructured interviewing, etc.

(Bryman, 1989)

In action research the researcher does not simply stand on the touchline watching. The researcher joins in the play.

By being a player in the action in the organization he or she is better able to appreciate what is going on, is better able to understand what it means to the other players, and is better able to contribute to the action. Action research holds that it is possible for the researcher to take an active part in the organization and, at the same time, observe the organization.

PARTICIPATIVE RESEARCH

Participative research goes one stage further. If it is possible for the outside researcher to be actively involved in the organization and at the same time research it, what is to prevent the clients from researching the organization while being actively involved in it?

The distinction between researcher and client, between observer and observed, is thus deliberately dissolved.

Some action research studies have endeavoured to make the clients into researchers. The logic is that the clients will be able to manage the problem better if they understand it better, which they can achieve by setting up their own research project. In effect the research has become **participative**, the clients participating in the research process.

> Action research assumes that any social phenomena are continually changing rather than static. Action research and the researcher are then seen as part of this change process itself. The following two features are normally part of the action research process.
>
> 1. A belief that the best way of learning about an organisation or social system is through attempting to change it, and this therefore should to some extent be the objective of the action researcher.
> 2. The belief that those people most likely to be affected by, or involved in implementing, these changes should as far as possible become involved in the research process itself.
>
> (Easterby-Smith, *et al.*, 1991)

Easterby-Smith's first point may be taken as a definition of action research. His second point is a definition of *participative research*, where the client organization's people are doing research on themselves.

EXAMPLES OF ACTION RESEARCH AND PARTICIPATIVE RESEARCH

Reg Revans led a project designed to improve communications in the hospitals in a way which involved both *participative research* and *action research*. There was a widespread feeling throughout much of the British National Health Service that communication was poor to the extent of being a major problem. Revans's team took an action research perspective in the sense that they set out to change the system at the same time that they studied it. It was viewed as a problem which affected and was caused by the hospital and the Health Service as a large system, rather than one easily isolated variable within it. Revans also chose to adopt a participative approach by getting the hospital staff to explore the problem, research it, and solve it for themselves.

With financial encouragement from the Ministry of Health, a programme of 'institutional learning' was established in a self-selected sample of ten London hospitals. Revans had deliberately decided not to tell the hospitals how they should organize themselves, and merely pointed out that morale and communications were important in this context. He suggested that senior persons should attend short courses in research techniques and then return to their hospitals to assist in instituting a series of internally formulated projects directed towards actual problems in the hospital. In this way Revans hoped to break the 'normal' natural history of a problem: typically, a problem emerges, is defined, and then allocated to experts who apply a procedure for its solution, thereby taking over the 'ownership' of the problem and inhibiting others from learning. In contrast, the medium through which hospital members were to learn more about their own and other persons' roles was through projects selected and undertaken by each hospital. It was expected that both the project and the result would contribute to the learning process. Here we see Revans's theory of education in action. The focus is upon the internal team, and the aim is to avoid the situation in which the external expert 'is bound to be seen by those in charge of the system as a threat to their institutionalized power'. . . . The approach is essentially non-directive. At the start of the programme each of the ten hospitals sent three senior members, one from each main group – administrative, nursing, and medical – to a three-day intensive course. Then each of their subordinates attended a one-month course emphasizing the importance of using the correct techniques for data collection in problem solving. It was planned that this course would have a major influence upon the nature of the projects undertaken, but there was a 'minimum of theory'. After the course they returned to their own hospitals and were encouraged to develop their own projects.

The design of the 'experiment' recognized that the concept of the projects was precarious, not least because the principal catalysts in the hospitals had no recognizable role-models to assist them. It was decided that this problem could be eased by arranging periodic meetings at which the project teams from the ten hospitals exchanged experiences. In addition they could gain special kinds of assistance and technical support from a 'central team' residing in London. Some of the hospitals employed undergraduate students to help in the collection and analysis of data. The central team comprised persons with a variety of skills and special experiences. They were not essentially academic in orientation, since this was not appropriate to the success of the concept. They did not control and direct, but acted as additional resources, working in part by establishing relationships with particular hospitals. It might be asked: 'Who were the main agents of organizational change?' Revans suggests that the central team was the primary change agent.

Within the ten hospitals the types of project formulated by the six-person teams varied widely, as did the influence of the teams. In practice they were not always integrated, and in the opinion of one student member, the whole exercise 'lacked skill and knowledge of the social sciences'.

An interesting facet of the project was the formation of a team to evaluate the impact of the 'experiment'. This is one of the few examples of action research in which there was concurrent observation and analysis.

(R. Revans, in Clark, 1979, pp. 42–3)

A second example of a research project which was both *participative research* and at the same time *action research* was conducted by Pasmore and Friedlander, cited in Bryman (1989, pp. 181–3).

The research site was a plant employing 335 people in the production of consumer electronics items. The authors describe the plant as imbued with a strong production orientation which largely emanated from the plant manager. Most jobs were simple and repetitive. The plant manager approached the authors to solicit their assistance in connection with a pervasive problem of work-related injuries, in that a large proportion of employees suffered from 'damage to muscles in the wrist, forearm and shoulder', a condition later identified as tenosynovitis. In some cases, the condition was very serious. The problem was worsening. Five years prior to the authors' involvement only two or three injuries per year were reported; two years later, there were almost forty; and at the time of the approach, the number of injuries was approaching eighty. The plant manager had commissioned a number of environmental studies of the plant and physiological examinations of the employees, but had never sought the employees' views of the causes of the problem. These studies were not very conclusive, but a number of patterns in the data (for example, some shifts were affected, but others were not) led to the conclusion that employees' reactions to work were more instrumental in the injury problem than the work itself, a view that prompted the manager to turn to social scientists for help.

Pasmore and Friedlander assembled various personnel (five employees, two foremen, a manager and themselves) to form the Studies and Communication Group whose function was 'to direct the investigation and convey results and recommendations for change to employees and management'. The group formulated a number of data collection strategies which were based on their delineation of various hunches about possible causes of the problem. The chief strategies were: open-ended interviews administered to employees, containing questions about their work, the climate of the firm and aspects of their injuries if they had experienced them; a questionnaire survey of employees, covering attitudes to their work and management, stress, working conditions, participation in decision-making, etc.; and participant observation by members of the group. These various studies helped the researchers to identify a constellation of factors that are summarized in the following passage:

> First, the necessary repetitive hand movements associated with tenosynovitis injury were present, compounded by tools out of adjustment, which caused victims to exert more pressure than they normally would. Second, the self-pressuring workforce [victims were found to be more conscientious and responsible than their peers] was unable to feel in control of its working conditions because of the organization's structure and management methods. Demands to increase productivity and unnecessarily tight supervisory control probably caused the tension that produced the initial injuries. Then, mass psychogenic contagion reactions occurred that resulted in large increases in stress and in the number of people affected. Injuries slowed production, which resulted in management's imposing even tighter controls and greater demands for production.
>
> (Pasmore and Friedlander, 1982, pp. 353, 354, 355)

On the basis of these findings, the Studies and Communication Group composed sixty-one recommendations for change, most of which were accepted by the plant manager. The data were fed back to all employees in conjunction with a list of actions that were to be introduced immediately to deal with the problem, including: continued adjustment of equipment; the continuation of the group; the establishment of an employee-management group to test possible work design changes in jobs which had been particularly prone to injuries; and the introduction of foreman training. Some months after the intervention had begun, two unforeseeable events occurred. The group concerned with work redesign discovered that the metal used for welds was of poor quality, and the employment of better quality materials enhanced the plant's productivity and product quality. Second, both the plant manager and supervisor of operations were replaced by new personnel. Pasmore and Friedlander argue that these changes may have been attributed to the action programme, and may have fostered a view that these new personnel would be more sensitive. The action research programme, in tandem with these unanticipated events, had a material impact; four years after the point at which the action research started, injuries were at a rate of only two or three per year. Further, materials usage and labour efficiency were enhanced.

Of course, the research lacks conventional standards of rigour in a number of ways. We do not know which particular changes had a beneficial impact on injuries, nor how far they would have had an impact without the unanticipated changes (although there was a clear decline in injuries prior to the occurrence of these unforeseeable events). Further, there is always the possibility that, in a situation in which there was widespread concern regarding an apparently intractable problem about which those affected were not consulted, *any* participative approach to problem-solving would have worked. On the other hand, as the authors note, more rigorous methods might have been a good deal less effective because they probably would not have involved the employees themselves in the search for a solution to the same degree.

This study exemplifies a number of characteristics of action research. The investigation is explicitly concerned with problem-solving, but also contributes to our understanding of industrial injuries and the effects of organization structure and job design on the experience of work. The research was carried out in a participative climate, in that the employees identified hunches and participated in the design and administration of the research instruments. Thus, action research contrasts with a consultant-client relationship, in which employees may have little or no participation in the nature and direction of the research effort, and in which there is little interest in the possible contribution of the investigation to the stock of knowledge. Further, the implementation stage is crucial, in that the fruits of research and proposed recommendations are rapidly introduced and their effects analysed (Bryman, 1984).

OLD PARADIGMS AND NEW PARADIGMS

The addition of *action research* and of *participative research* allows us to study areas which the older paradigm of positivist-empiricist research could not reach. It would not have been possible within the positivist tradition to get the research subjects involved in the research studying themselves. But then it was not necessary since positivism originated in the physical sciences where research subjects are usually inanimate objects. Positrons are not known to be self-reflexive. Electrons do not show much interest in the design of experiments to study electrons.

The older paradigms of positivism, empiricism, statistical analysis, hypothesis testing, experimental research have developed a whole battery of testing to check whether the conclusions drawn from such research approaches are reliable as valid knowledge. Statistics offers a range of formulae to test whether the results of a statistical analysis are significant; whether a sample is large enough to be representative and so on. Hypothesis testing and experimental research have developed the use of the control group and of repeatability under controlled laboratory conditions as a 'means of stopping the researchers misleading themselves' about their conclusions.

In moving beyond the older paradigms with their well-established tests of validity, the researcher has to proceed with caution. The new paradigm methods of action research and participative research need to be accompanied by tests of validity no less rigorous and no less reliable than those that serve to test conclusions drawn from the physical sciences. The question: How do you know? is just as important in the development of management knowledge as anywhere – the validity tests are still being developed. They include those discussed earlier, namely generalizability, intersubjectivity, critical self-awareness, repetition, verisimilitude, and theoretical congruence. These are at best tools to assist the researcher, never to replace that person. They equip the researcher with a useful repertoire for acquiring new insights, new knowledge and for assessing the extent to which it is trustworthy. But always the researcher must be on guard to ask.

How do I know?
and
How do I know that I know?

NEW PARADIGM RESEARCH

A new school of research methodology is evolving, variously called 'endogenous research', or simply 'new paradigm research'. Like a new movement in art it begins with a blast on its trumpet, a declaration of belief.

> Thousands of researchers down the years have started on projects they really believed in, and which embodied ideas they really believed in, and which embodied ideas they really cared about. But too often these projects got pared down and chopped about and falsified in the process of getting approval, and the researchers got progressively more disillusioned and frustrated as they have gone on. Thousands of researchers have ended their research soured and disappointed and hurt and cynical. It doesn't have to be this way. Research doesn't have to be another brick in the wall. It is obscene to take a young researcher who actually wants to know more about people, and divert them into manipulating 'variables', counting 'behaviours', observing

'responses' and all the rest of the ways in which people are falsified and fragmented. If we want to know about people, we have to encourage them to be who they are, and resist all attempts to make them – or ourselves – into something we are not, but which is more easily observable, or countable, or manipulable.

Someone has got to be the next generation of great social scientists – the women and men who are going to break the ground of new knowledge for human growth and development to the next stage. You, the reader, might be one of them – Why not?

(Reason and Rowan, 1981)

After that splendid rallying call, the new paradigm researchers carry on, as is the custom with a new movement in art, with an almighty kick at what they do not like, which naturally is what went before. Since they do this with such gusto, let us not interrupt them.

But there is a great deal of orthodoxy which we do oppose, and which we believe is very open to criticism. Let us very briefly look at some of the things we object to.

Model of the person. People are seen as isolable from their normal social contexts, as units to be moved into research designs, manipulated, and moved out again. People are seen as alienated and self-contained, stripped of all that gives their action meaning, and in this way they are trivialized.

Positivism. The whole language of 'operational definitions', 'dependent and independent variables', and so forth is highly suspect. It assumes that people can be reduced to a set of variables which are somehow equivalent across persons and across situations, which doesn't make much sense to us.

Reductionism. Studying variables rather than persons or groups or communities is a flight from understanding in depth, a flight from knowing human phenomena as wholes. It means that the person, group, community *as such* is never known.

Reification. Processes are continually turned into things. Test results are continually turned into things. None of this is philosophically defensible, and a lot of it is morally indefensible too.

Quantophrenia. There is too much measurement going on. Some things which are numerically precise are not true; and some things which are not numerical are true. Orthodox research produces results which are statistically significant but humanly insignificant; in human inquiry it is much better to be deeply interesting than accurately boring.

Testing. Intelligence tests and other tests of aptitude and personality are culturally biased and are used in unfair ways. There can be no fair tests within an unfair society.

Deception. There is too much lying going on. Unnecessary withholding of information comes naturally to many orthodox researchers. There is an arrogance about this which does not commend itself. Research is a game which two or more can play.

Debriefing. There is an assumption that a bad experience can somehow be wiped out by a brief and superficial explanation. But experience cannot be removed in that way. We should not inflict harm on people in the first place; good research means never having to say you are sorry.

Contamination. Orthodox research tries to eliminate real life, but it cannot do so. Researchers give off all sorts of messages in all kinds of ways. They try to direct scenes on the research stage, but they are actually part of the play. The eye-blink reflex is natural, but measuring it is a social situation.

Sampling. Large messages are extracted from small samples. Broad generalizations are made from unrepresentative bases. Old paradigm research often breaks its own rules in this area, quite regularly and shamelessly.

Detachment. Researchers actually try to know as little as possible about the phenomenon under study – it might affect the results if they knew too much. This is exactly the opposite of an approach which could do justice to human action.

Conservatism. Because of its lack of interest in the real social context, old paradigm research continually gets co-opted by those who want to prop up those who run the existing system. It studies those at the bottom while holding up its hands for money to those at the top. Thus in fact it serves to keep those at the bottom right there, and those at the top there.

Bigness. Researchers in the old mode are continually asking for bigger and better instruments, bigger and better samples, bigger and better premises, bigger and better travelling expenses. This turns research into big business, and makes it more likely to be the servant of those who can afford to pay big money: it answers *their* questions.

Low utilization. It is often remarked that large organizations pay for more research than they need, and then use only a tiny proportion of it. Sometimes questions are put to confirm decisions which have already been made. Because the whole process is alienated, there are few connections and very little commitment, and the people who receive the report may indeed be very different from those who commissioned it.

Language. Research reports are written for the expert, and have heavy constraints on the way they have to be written up for journal publication. The effect is to mystify the public, hiding common sense notions actually being employed. Another effect is that conformity is rewarded more highly than creativity.

Pressures. Journal publication policies and funding policies of grant-awarding bodies put severe pressure on for safe, respectable research. Fads come in from time to time and offer a band-wagon to climb upon. Researchers are continually short of time and funds, continually looking for projects which mean a minimum of disturbance to the even tenor of their ways. Research gets more and more specialized, less and less to do with anything real.

Determinism. Old paradigm research holds to a determinist model, where the independent variable coerces the dependent variable into performing correctly. Belief in determinism leads to the setting up of coercive (master-slave) relations in the laboratory, where there is an alienated relationship between the experimenter and the subject.

Scientific fairy-tale. Textbooks which have a chapter on the scientific method have various ideas about what this includes, but all of them are equally dogmatic about the three or four points they mention. What they put forward, however, is a storybook image, which does not correspond with the way in which science is actually carried on. In real science there are norms and counternorms: for example, in real science it is often considered highly praiseworthy to be unwilling to change one's opinions in the light of the latest piece of evidence; lack of humility is highly valued; bias is freely acknowledged; there is a lot of interest in how discoveries might be applied; there is a great deal of emphasis on the importance of intuitive judgement. So the textbook versions falsify science, and dominate education.

So much for the negative case. We are not going to elaborate it further because these arguments have been made many times and are easily available; all these separate points taken together add up to a powerful indictment (Israel and Tajfel, 1972; P. Brown, 1973; Joynson, 1974; Kamin, 1974; Heather, 1976; Argyris, 1968a; Friedlander, 1968; Bass, 1974).

(Reason and Rowan, 1981, pp. xiv-xvi)

That clearly is what they are against. What are they for?

COOPERATIVE INQUIRY

John Heron argues for cooperative inquiry in which researcher and subject cooperate. Research subjects, i.e. the people to be studied, 'contribute directly to hypothesis-making, to formulating the final conclusions, and to what goes on in between'. The subject may have a strong hand in the creative thinking of the project design or less involvement being merely informed. Heron contrasts this research approach with

> the traditional social science experiment or study in which the subjects are kept naive about the research propositions and make no contribution at all to formulation at the stage of hypothesis-making, at the stage of final conclusions, or anywhere in between. In the extreme, and still popular form of this approach, the inquiry is all on the side of the researcher, and the action being inquired into is all on the side of the subject.
>
> (J. Heron, in Reason and Rowan, 1981)

ENDOGENOUS RESEARCH

> Each culture is studied by its insiders using endogenous epistemology, methodology, research design, and with endogenously relevant focus.
>
> (Maruyama, in Reason and Rowan, 1981)

The logic underlying endogenous research is that to understand a culture one can only make sense of it through the eyes of its people. An outsider from another culture will bring the wrong frames of reference to it and consequently may misunderstand it. One sees this regularly in dealings between two different national cultures. A director of Shell tells a true story which illustrates this point well.

David on joining Shell was sent to Thailand. He was determined to learn the Thai language. He found a teacher at the local mission school and learned the language. Later he observed that when Western colleagues visited Thailand they were entertained at nightclubs and at places of suitably ill repute. David, on the other hand, was taken to see only temples and religious shrines. It was not easy to inquire without giving offence why this should be. As he explains, when your host has taken trouble to arrange a visit for you to a religious edifice, you can hardly ask him why he has not taken you to the red light district. Eventually David discovered that the problem lay in the type of Thai that he had learned. It seemed that there was Royal Thai spoken in the courts, bazaar Thai spoken in bartering in the markets. And there was Religious Thai, which is what he had learned at the mission school. Because David's every word was Religious Thai his hosts took him to be a very religious person and entertained him accordingly. What he was saying was the equivalent of 'Yea verily brethren I say unto thee . . .'. Not perceiving what he was saying through endogenous (i.e. native) ears, David could not understand how his hosts perceived him.

A similar problem arises in comparing the financial performance of US or UK companies with companies from France or Germany. On the basis of the published figures in the accounts one may conclude that the Anglo-Saxon company makes more or less profit than its counterpart in mainland Europe. That would be a mistake. Profit means something different in the different cultures. It is calculated differently. The purpose for which it is calculated is different. That difference has to do with other national differences such as the roles of bank and stock markets in financing companies, the nature of shareholders and culture traditions concerning the obligations to the next generation. Without understanding these factors the foreign observer cannot properly understand what the profit figure really signifies. It is an output of a system that is foreign to the observer. In order to understand the meaning of a native's behaviour the researcher has to understand what it means to that native, seen through his eyes, given meaning by his endogenous (i.e. native) culture. To achieve this it may be necessary to involve the locals when researching their lives, organizations, cultures.

> Endogenous research is conceptualised, designed, and conducted by researchers who are insiders of the culture, using their own epistemology and their own structure of relevance.
>
> (Maruyama, in Reason and Rowan, 1981)

This insider's insight may be combined with the outsider researcher's point of view to give what Maruyama calls a binocular view of the situation.

RESPECTING THE OBJECTIVES OF RESEARCHER AND RESEARCHED

Since researcher and research subject are both engaged in the research it seems reasonable that both parties' objectives are respected. They may not be identical. Maruyama quotes the example of some research in a prison. The prison inmates felt that the research should serve their purposes – which included making the public aware of their living and working conditions, their physical and mental treatment – to bring pressure to improve vocational training facilities, etc. The inmates believed that the researchers were only interested in their own pay-offs: testing their pet theories, producing publications, gaining a reputation for themselves. In a cooperative inquiry all objectives require to be recognized and satisfied. That has a relevance to many management projects where the hidden agendas can be large. The research subjects may, for example, have to manage their image within their own organization and ensure that the research aids, and does not damage, that image. They may use the researcher as a way of passing information or a point of view to other people in the organization. Research inside organizations often takes place in a political context. Research subjects, as well as researchers and clients, have their own ends to serve.

IN CONCLUSION

Any project seeks to study a situation, reach a conclusion, make a recommendation. It is of paramount importance that the conclusions are reliable and trustworthy. The conclusions can only be relied upon if the research has been well carried out, and the conclusions and recommendations rigorously examined. There exists a whole body of science, called **research methodology**, which serves to provide the researcher with a wide choice of means for investigating the subject, warns of the strengths and weaknesses of each of these means, and provides a rigorous batch of tests to ensure that the outcomes of the research are reliable. A researcher who undertakes an inquiry without a proper understanding of research methodology is not equipped to proceed. It is the equivalent of sailing out onto the deepest ocean without charts, compass, navigation equipment, or communications. It constitutes wilful negligence, a danger to all concerned.

The sources of research methodology and of the tool kit available to the management researcher are many. The several branches of the physical sciences, the social sciences, and more recently management research itself provide a wide range of tools and techniques. To use them effectively requires some skill and study allied to common sense and a manager's judgement. These chapters have described the range of techniques available and how to use them. Most important is to understand why they are needed and what purpose they serve. The references at the end of the book show where each of the techniques can be examined in greater detail and depth.

PART THREE
Classic Examples of
Management Research

Now let us examine some of the outstanding examples of management research.

TOM PETERS and BOB WATERMAN set out to discover why the most successful companies in America were excellent. Were there generalizable secrets of success? Could we learn from their success stories and achieve similar success in other companies by following the lessons learned from them?

They studied America's most successful companies in depth, publishing their results in the book *In Search of Excellence*. The book has become a best seller. The authors have grown rich.

MICHAEL PORTER of Harvard Business School set out to understand how industries work. What is it that causes an industry to be profitable? Why is it that in other industries all the players have to struggle to make a living? What in effect are the forces that drive industrial competition?

Porter's approach was to create a model of how an industry might work. An economist by training, his model argued from first principles that the key relationships were between buyers, competitors, and suppliers. Understand the relative bargaining power of those competing groups and we have understood the industry. Having created the model, Porter then set out to test it, to see if his model was a useful representation of reality.

Porter published his research, and grew rich and famous on the proceeds.

GEERT HOFSTEDE's research project was to discover a means of understanding why people of different national cultures differed in the way they did business, in their expectations of each other and of business partners. Having worked with managers of many nationalities Hofstede was well aware of how easily business deals and interpersonal relations break down through mutual non-comprehension. Hofstede set out to seek a key to the mysteries. Was it possible to identify how a Frenchman would differ in his expectations and behaviour in business from a Japanese? Could one go further and identify underlying causes and belief systems?

Hofstede studied the responses of thousands of managers of scores of nationalities to a lengthy questionnaire. He found that a manager's reaction to many situations was to a large extent determined by nationality. The response was largely predictable and explainable.

Hofstede published his findings in the book *Culture's Consequences*.

Here we have three outstanding examples of management research. All three have been widely adopted by practising managers throughout the world. At least two of these projects are reported to have made their authors into millionaires, which is one measure of success.

Let us examine them to see how they did it, how they carried out their research.

Let us examine them from the point of view of the external examiners. By putting ourselves in the position of the examiners and subjecting these three projects to scrutiny and assessment we shall gain a better understanding of how we ourselves will be examined on our projects when our time comes.

In Search of Excellence

9

As we have seen, the research begins by identifying a **project idea**. This would be an area of sufficient interest for the researcher to devote time and energy in its pursuit. The project idea has to be of interest to a wider audience. Research is not an exercise only in introspection. There have to be benefits for a wider community.

The project idea has then to be refined into a **research question**. The research question is the key question that the entire research project is designed to answer.

Once the researchers know the precise question they want to answer, the next stage is to decide on the **research methodology**. How are we going to do the research? How are we going to find the answers to this research question? What information do we need, and how are we going to get it?

These are precisely the same stages that we all have to go through in designing our research projects. They are brought together into the **project plan**, first encountered in Chapter 1.

Let us follow Peters and Waterman through each stage of their research project to see how they have handled each stage of the project.

THE PROJECT IDEA

In Search of Excellence is subtitled *Lessons from America's best-run companies*, which defines the objectives of the project clearly. The essential objective of the project was to study the best-run companies in America to discover why they were successful. What were they doing that made them successful? Could the recipes for success be identified and made known to other companies to copy?

The idea for the research did not simply pop up ready made. It grew out of many different experiences and of mulling over the idea that some companies are better than others. Some companies are known to be good companies. Why? What makes them good? How do they do it? Peters and Waterman had worked in a number of companies. They had been consultants with McKinsey and Company, working with a variety of clients. They had burrowed in the theory, in books touching on corporate excellence, swapped experiences and anecdotes of good and bad companies with colleagues. Just like other researchers they had to spend time playing with the subject area of interest, thinking about it, reading around it, leaving it for a while, before it began to blend into a workable shape.

Peters and Waterman recount a number of stories of how gradually the idea of corporate excellence came to catch their attention.

> We had decided after dinner to spend a second night in Washington. Our business day had taken us beyond the last convenient flight out. We had no hotel reservations, but were near the new Four Seasons, had stayed there once before and liked it. As we walked through the lobby wondering how best to plead our case for a room, we braced for the usual chilly shoulder accorded to latecomers. To our astonishment the concierge looked up, smiled, called us by name, and asked how we were. She remembered our names! We knew in a flash why in the space of a brief year the Four Seasons had become the place to stay in the District and was a rare first-year holder of the venerated four star rating.

That particular experience could have sparked off all sorts of research ideas. Or none at all. It did spark off an idea for Peters and Waterman because they had already been mulling over ideas of corporate excellence. As the old Buddhist saying observes: Enlightenment comes to the prepared mind.

Another anecdote concerns Boeing.

> We were talking to a group of Boeing executives about our research and making the point that excellent companies seem to take all sorts of special trouble to foster, nourish, and care for what we call product champions – those individuals who believe so strongly in their ideas that they take it on themselves to damn the bureaucracy and manoeuvre their projects through the system and out to the customer . . .

They told us the story about how Boeing really won the contracts for the swept wing B–47, which was later to become the highly successful first commercial jet, the 707. They also told the story of how Boeing really won the contract for the B–52 . . .

These were both fine tales of little teams of people going to extraordinary lengths to get results on behalf of a truly unusual corporation.

Again there are several possible themes that could be grown into a project idea. The use of anecdotes, war stories, company mythology, tales of success and near catastrophe as a means of identifying company strategy, culture, and competence. The importance of product champions, how to nurture and use them. The way to create and use a project team. A study of motivation, of the contrast of project teams, sometimes called skunk works, and the bureaucracy. There are large numbers of good projects floating around in the Peters and Waterman book just waiting for someone to pick them up and refine them.

THE RESEARCH QUESTION

Eventually Peters and Waterman's thinking crystallized on what it was that they wanted to do: find the reasons why some companies were excellent. That is the **research question**. As usual, once we have the research question clear in our minds we also know how we can do it. The question is: 'Why are some companies excellent?' Therefore it follows that the researchers must first identify those companies that are excellent. Then find out why they are excellent. Then examine the recipes for excellence of each of these companies to find patterns common to all, or to most of them.

RESEARCH METHODOLOGY

Q. *How are we going to do it?*
A. Well, first we identify the excellent companies.
Q. *How?*
A. We ask lots of people which companies they think of as excellent.
Q. *How do we know that they really are excellent?*
A. We devise a battery of tests to check that they really are excellent according to many objective, factual measurable criteria, e.g.
  - compound asset growth over a 20-year period up to today
  - compound equity growth over the same period
  - the average ratio of market value to book value
  - average return on total capital over the 20-year period
  - average return on equity over that period
  - average return on sales over that period
  - views of industry experts on excellence
  - views of industry experts on innovativeness.

When inevitably the researchers are asked, 'How do you know that these companies which you have studied really are excellent?', they have a powerful answer ready.

The next problem is how to discover from these chosen companies why they are excellent. The researchers chose to use intense structured interviews in the companies. This was supplemented by study of press coverage, annual reports and similar secondary data. They 'also studied some under-achieving companies for purposes of comparison, but we didn't concentrate much on this, as we felt we had plenty of insight into under-achievement through our combined twenty-four years in the management consulting business'.

They were careful to ensure that their sixty-three companies were not all drawn from a small sector of industry but were representative of most industries: high technology, consumer goods, general industrial, services, project management, resource based.

The problem still remains of what questions to ask in the structured interviews. The respondents could talk about anything: length of service, pay, family connections, car policy, canteen, bureaucracy, holidays, anything. The researchers had to decide what questions they would ask. They would have to ask the same questions to all interviewees in all companies and ask them in the same way. Otherwise they could make no comparisons or conclusions from the data. Here we have the problem of the interplay of theory and data. The researchers want to hear what the company executives think are the reasons for their companies' success. But to obtain their answers they have to ask them questions. The questions are chosen by the researchers on the basis of the researchers' ideas about what is important. How do the researchers know what questions to ask?

The researchers have a theory.

> We had used the 7-S framework as the basic structuring device for our interviews and hence chose the same framework as a way of communicating our conclusions.

The 7-S framework is shown in Fig. 9.1. Its main message is that in a corporation structure, systems, strategy, staff, skills, style, and shared values are all interrelated. To change one – strategy, for example – it may be necessary to make supporting changes in the others.

> Our research told us that any intelligent approach to organizing had to encompass, and treat as interdependent, at least seven variables: structure, strategy, people, management style, systems and procedures, guiding concepts and shared values (culture) and the present and hoped-for corporate strengths and skills.

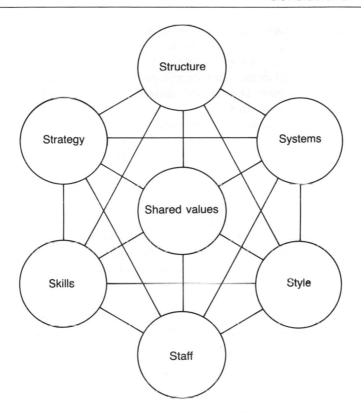

CONCLUSIONS

The researchers derived eight principles of management from their project. These eight principles were the reasons why the companies studied were successful. They are summarized below by Peters and Waterman.

The eight attributes that emerged to characterize most nearly the distinction of the excellent, innovative companies go as follows:

1. *A bias for action*, for getting on with it. Even though these companies may be analytical in their approach to decision making, they are not paralyzed by that fact (as so many others seem to be). In many of these companies the standard operating procedure is 'Do it, fix it, try it.' Says a Digital Equipment Corporation senior executive, for example, 'When we've got a big problem here, we grab ten senior guys and stick them in a room for a week. They come up with an answer *and* implement it.' Moreover, the companies are experimenters supreme. Instead of allowing 250 engineers and marketers

to work on a new product in isolation for fifteen months, they form bands of 5 to 25 and test ideas out on a customer, often with inexpensive prototypes, within a matter of weeks. What is striking is the host of practical devices the excellent companies employ, to maintain corporate fleetness of foot and counter the stultification that almost inevitably comes with size.

2. *Close to the customer*. These companies learn from the people they serve. They provide unparalleled quality, service, and reliability – things that work and last. They succeed in differentiating – *à la* Frito-Lay (potato chips), Maytag (washers), or Tupperware – the most commodity-like products. IBM's marketing vice president, Francis G. (Buck) Rodgers, says, 'It's a shame that, in so many companies, whenever you get good service, it's an exception.' Not so at the excellent companies. Everyone gets into the act. Many of the innovative companies got their best product ideas from customers. That comes from listening, intently and regularly.

3. *Autonomy and entrepreneurship*. The innovative companies foster many leaders and many innovators throughout the organization. They are a hive of what we've come to call champions; 3M has been described as 'so intent on innovation that its essential atmosphere seems not like that of a large corporation but rather a loose network of laboratories and cubbyholes populated by feverish inventors and dauntless entrepreneurs who let their imaginations fly in all directions.' They don't try to hold everyone on so short a rein that he can't be creative. They encourage practical risk taking, and support good tries. They follow Fletcher Byrom's ninth commandment: 'Make sure you generate a reasonable number of mistakes.'

4. *Productivity through people*. The excellent companies treat the rank and file as the root source of quality and productivity gain. They do not foster we/they labor attitudes or regard capital investment as the fundamental source of efficiency improvement. As Thomas J. Watson, Jr., said of his company, 'IBM's philosophy is largely contained in three simple beliefs. I want to begin with what I think is the most important: *our respect for the individual*. This is a simple concept, but in IBM it occupies a major portion of management time.' Texas Instruments' chairman Mark Shepherd talks about it in terms of every worker being 'seen as a source of ideas, not just acting as a pair of hands'; each of his more than 9,000 People Involvement Program, or PIP, teams (TI's quality circles) does contribute to the company's sparkling productivity record.

5. *Hands-on, value driven*. Thomas Watson, Jr., said that 'the basic philosophy of an organization has far more to do with its achievements than do technological or economic resources, organizational structure, innovation and timing.' Watson and HP's William Hewlett

are legendary for walking the plant floors. McDonald's Ray Kroc regularly visits stores and assesses them on the factors the company holds dear, Q.S.C. & V. (Quality, Service, Cleanliness, and Value).

6. *Stick to the knitting.* Robert W. Johnson, former Johnson & Johnson chairman, put it this way: 'Never acquire a business you don't know how to run.' Or as Edward G. Harness, past chief executive at Procter & Gamble, said, 'This company has never left its base. We seek to be anything but a conglomerate.' While there were a few exceptions, the odds for excellent performance seem strongly to favor those companies that stay reasonably close to businesses they know.

7. *Simple form, lean staff.* As big as most of the companies we have looked at are, none when we looked at it was formally run with a matrix organization structure, and some which had tried that form had abandoned it. The underlying structural forms and systems in the excellent companies are elegantly simple. Top-level staffs are lean; it is not uncommon to find a corporate staff of fewer than 100 people running multi-billion-dollar enterprises.

8. *Simultaneous loose-tight properties.* The excellent companies are both centralized and decentralized. For the most part, as we have said, they have pushed autonomy down to the shop floor or product development team. On the other hand, they are fanatic centralists around the few core values they hold dear. 3M is marked by barely organized chaos surrounding its product champions. Yet one analyst argues, 'The brainwashed members of an extremist political sect are no more conformist in their central beliefs.' At Digital the chaos is so rampant that one executive noted, 'Damn few people know who they work for.' Yet Digital's fetish for reliability is more rigidly adhered to than any outsider could imagine.

(In Search of Excellence, pp. 13–16)

A PRE-EXAMINATION OF *IN SEARCH OF EXCELLENCE*

Now let us put ourselves in the position of being external examiners.

If Peters and Waterman were due to appear before us for a *viva voce* examination on their research, what questions would we ask them? What are the areas of their research that we should wish to probe? What is our initial judgement of their research?

BEFORE READING THE NEXT SECTION, decide for yourself. Use the example of Peters and Waterman to develop your skill in critical evaluation of research. Once you have that skill you can apply it to your own research and, as a result, produce far better work.

EXAMINING *IN SEARCH OF EXCELLENCE*

To be able to stand back from your research and take a critical, objective view of it, as though you were a detached observer, is a useful skill to acquire. You develop the skill to see your work as others, including examiners and clients, see it.

That **helicopter** quality, as it is sometimes called, is a valuable skill in any situation. It is the ability to take part in the situation as an active involved player and at the same time to see it in perspective, as though you were able to step out of the scene and view it from above. Hence the helicopter image.

Bert Juch, in his research on what distinguishes an outstanding manager from the merely competent, identified the helicopter quality as the real distinguishing characteristic. In Shell, for example, Bert found that all good managers had the standard tools of the manager's art such as marketing, finance, HR, IT, etc. They also had the skill to integrate all of these diverse areas and use them as aspects of one unified whole, which is general management. The real high flyers are those who can add to these skills the helicopter quality. That, according to Bert's research, more than any other single quality marks out the special and potentially great manager from those who are just good to middling.

One can develop the critical awareness, the detached observer's helicopter view, most easily by practising first on another person's work. Then when we are comfortable with the approach we apply it to our own.

Let us begin with Peters and Waterman's *In Search of Excellence* research.

WHAT HAVE THEY ACTUALLY DONE?

To get to grips with any piece of research which you are examining it is useful as a first step to summarize what they have actually done. We are seeking to identify in a few short sentences the **logic of the research**. What Peters and Waterman present to us are a few clearly logical steps from research question to conclusion. Their research question was: 'Why are the most successful companies successful?' Can we identify the reasons for their success and make it available for others to learn from? Their conclusion is: Yes. We can identify the reasons for their success. Here they are.

What then is the **logic** which takes them from research question to conclusion?

1. Identify a large number of successful companies.
2. Identify why they are successful.
3. Interpret the data. Seek out recurring themes and recipes common

to many of the companies which explain their success. These are the eight attributes.

4. These are the reasons for success. Companies that do likewise shall be likewise successful.

Once we have set out the *logic* of their research it is easier to ask insightful questions about it. (*N.B.* This is a useful technique to apply to your own research.)

- What is the research question?
- What is the conclusion?
- What is the logic that takes you and the audience from question to conclusion?

When you have the research question, conclusion and the logic of the research, interrogate it, as we shall now do with Peters and Waterman's work.

Logic Step 1. Identify a large number of successful companies

Why these companies? Are there enough of them to allow us to draw generalizable conclusions? Sixty-three is a lot. Are they representative?

NO. They are representative of very successful companies. BUT they are not representative of all companies. They have been chosen precisely because they are not representative. They are different. They are outstandingly successful.

Here we have a possible flaw in the logic. The implied logic is: DEC is a successful company. DEC attributes its success to certain things which it does. Therefore other companies which copy these certain things shall be successful also. That does not necessarily follow logically. DEC has offices in Reading and Geneva. Some DEC people consider these office locations to be very useful. But no one suggests that all businesses including the Rotherham steelworks and the Brixham Fisherman's Co-operative should relocate to Reading and Geneva to increase their success. An absurd example, not from Peters and Waterman, but it makes the point.

There is a question of *logic* about whether lessons learned from companies selected because they are different from the mass can be generalized to the mass. Characteristics of one group (the group of very successful companies) may not apply equally to another group (the group of less successful but ambitious companies).

Examiners probe here.

Logic Step 2. Identify why they are successful

How have Peters and Waterman identified why they are successful? **How do they know** that these are the reasons for success? And not just the sales pitch of the sales director, plus the unctions of the public relations office, and the homespun philosophy of an ageing managing director?

Imagine you were conducting this research yourself. Think of a company you know to be successful. How would you find out why it is successful? Who would you ask? The chief executive or the shopfloor? They might both give different answers. And what questions would you ask them? 'Excuse me, sir, tell me why you are successful?'

Peters and Waterman keep rather quiet in their book *In Search of Excellence* on how they identified the reasons for success.

Examiners could be expected to ask lots of probing questions at the *viva voce* examination about this.

Logic Step 3. Interpret the data

Peters and Waterman have accumulated vast numbers of answers to questions from many people in many companies. Now they have to make sense of all the data. What does it all mean? How have they made the jump from thousands of interview reports to the eight attributes?

This is our familiar area of the interplay of theory and data, the relationship between subjective and objective in research.

All the people interviewed did not reply with one mighty voice: 'Our success is attributable to the eight attributes.' They had presumably never heard of the eight attributes until years later when Peters and Waterman published their book. Instead they said something else. Lots of different people said different things. The researchers had to make sense of all this jumble of data; to distil from it a few useful recurring themes. Exactly how they made sense of the data mountain is an area that examiners and researchers should probe. It may contain problems.

Logic Step 4. These are the reasons for success. Companies that do likewise shall be likewise successful

That is the implied conclusion. The probable reason why millions of people bought the book, though Peters and Waterman stop slightly short of promising success to all imitators.

Is there any evidence that a less successful company will become more successful if it copies the eight attributes? No. None that I know of as yet.

Logic Step 4 is unproved and untested. That does not make Peters and Waterman's research valueless. They have done a useful job in identifying what some people in some successful companies think is the reason for their past success. That is a useful piece of descriptive research. But it remains to be seen whether other companies can become more successful by copying the eight attributes. That would take another major piece of research to find out.

It is not even clear whether the reasons identified for past success in these selected successful companies will keep them successful in the future. A follow-up study ten years later found that, of the sixty-three successful companies selected by Peters and Waterman, less than a quarter were successful ten years later, measured on the same criteria. Again this does not render Peters and Waterman's work worthless. They identified something. They told us something interesting and helpful. It was not the end of all research; just a step along the way. If we want to know why the companies fell from grace, that is another research project.

Now that you have a feel for how to examine a research project bear it in mind while we see what Michael Porter has been doing.

Industry Analysis and Generic Strategies

10

The best-known theorist in strategy at the end of the 1980s and early 1990s is Michael Porter, Professor at Harvard Business School. His fame is firmly established on two management research projects, one on Industry Analysis, one on Generic Strategies, in his book *Competitive Advantage*. As a result of these projects Porter is said to earn vast fortunes every year from sales of the videos and books that report his project findings and from the resultant consultancy for corporate clients. Porter is living proof that good management research can earn a fortune.

Porter's research methodology is very different from Peters and Waterman. They study sixty-three companies and draw inferences from their data. He, by contrast, uses economic and game theory models to construct a theoretical model of how an industry might be structured, then goes out and tests it with actual industries. Peters and Waterman are using inductive reasoning; Porter uses deductive reasoning. In fact the difference is not so pure and absolute. Peters and Waterman, in looking at their data, already have some notions, some prior theories that help them to look at it. Porter, when creating his concepts and theories in his intellectual fortress, has already benefited from substantial practical experience. The interplay of theorizing and of gathering fresh data is continuous. The difference between induction and deduction is a matter of emphasis.

THE PROJECT IDEA

Porter's theoretical models 'grow out of my research and practice in competitive strategy over the past decade'. His thinking around the subject has been aided by cross-fertilization of ideas from Harvard colleagues.

I had a great deal of help. . . . The Harvard Business School has provided a uniquely fertile environment in which to explore this topic. I have drawn heavily on the multi-disciplinary tradition at the School as well as the close connections between research and practice that exists there.

Notice again, as with Peters and Waterman, project ideas, insights, and tentative theories develop naturally from exploring in and around the broad subject area. Students, when first faced with the need to do a project, often wail: 'I don't know what to do for a project.' Of course they don't. Even Porter did not know what to do for a project until he had spent a lot of time exploring the several areas that interested him, reading widely, discussing with colleagues, thinking about potentially interesting questions, trying out ideas, discarding some, pursuing others.

By the time Porter is ready to write the project report and the book he has put all his thoughts into as logical and as clear an order as necessary to convey them to the reader. It should not be assumed that the research was always so organized. For much of the time he probably had very little idea of where his research would eventually take him. Even the best organized research is still an exploration of unknown territory.

THE RESEARCH QUESTION

Porter sets out to tackle two questions:

1. What is it that makes an industry attractive or unattractive?
2. How does a company achieve a position of relative competitive advantage in its industry?

Why these two questions in particular?

Porter has a long cultural and theoretical history which has resulted in these two questions. Some he is explicit about; some has to be inferred from his writing. In part the questions spring from the concerns of people working in the field. In part, too, the questions spring from Porter's own mind, from his previous study, informed by economic theory and game theory.

The conceptual underpinnings of Porter's models are summarized by Porter, as follows:

Competition is at the core of the success or failure of firms. Competition determines the appropriateness of a firm's activities that can contribute to its performance, such as innovations, a cohesive culture, or good implementation. Competitive strategy is the search for a favourable competitive position in an industry, the fundamental arena in which competition occurs. Competitive strategy aims to establish a profitable and sustainable position against the forces that determine industry competition.

Two central questions underlie the choice of competitive strategy. The first is the attractiveness of industries for long-term profitability and the factors that determine it. . . . The second central question in competitive strategy is the determinants of relative competitive position within an industry.

(Porter, 1985)

Given that world view the research questions follow logically. If the reader does not share Porter's world view, or feels that the factors included in Porter's model of the world are not all of the most important factors to be taken into account in formulating strategy, then the two questions posed by Porter may not seem the most important. The research questions are a product of the researcher's world view – with Porter as with any researcher.

INDUSTRY ANALYSIS

Porter proposes a model for understanding any industry. There are five forces which shape the industry:

- competitors
- buyers (i.e. customers)
- suppliers
- the threat of substitutes
- the threat of new entrants.

In any industry, if one looks at the relative strengths of each of these five forces, one can discover how attractive or unattractive the industry will be and, consequently, how profitable it will be. The model allows the reader to draw a map of the relative strength of each of the player groups in the industry, showing, for example, how powerful suppliers are in relation to the company. By mapping where the company has strengths and weaknesses relative to other players, the model can guide the company's strategy to repair its weaknesses and capitalize on its strengths.

The full Industry Analysis model is shown in Fig. 10.1.

Having established the model the next stage is empirical testing. The model may seem elegant and logical as a theory. Does it work in practice?

Porter presents his evidence in his videos more than in his books. In the videos he uses Industry Analysis to help the viewer to analyse and

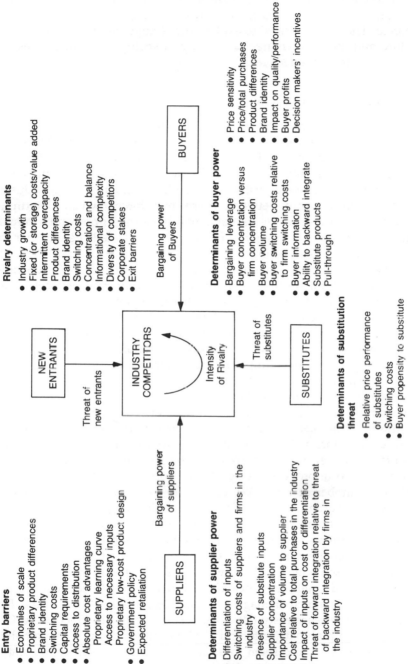

Entry barriers

- Economies of scale
- Proprietary product differences
- Brand identity
- Switching costs
- Capital requirements
- Access to distribution
- Absolute cost advantages
  Proprietary learning curve
  Access to necessary inputs
  Proprietary low-cost product design
- Government policy
- Expected retaliation

Rivalry determinants

- Industry growth
- Fixed (or storage) costs/value added
- Intermittent overcapacity
- Product differences
- Brand identity
- Switching costs
- Concentration and balance
- Informational complexity
- Diversity of competitors
- Corporate stakes
- Exit barriers

Determinants of supplier power

- Differentiation of inputs
- Switching costs of suppliers and firms in the industry
- Presence of substitute inputs
- Supplier concentration
- Importance of volume to supplier
- Cost relative to total purchases in the industry
- Impact of inputs on cost or differentiation
- Threat of forward integration relative to threat of backward integration by firms in the industry

Determinants of buyer power

- Bargaining leverage
- Buyer concentration versus firm concentration
- Buyer volume
- Buyer switching costs relative to firm switching costs
- Buyer information
- Ability to backward integrate
- Substitute products
- Pull-through

- Price sensitivity
- Price/total purchases
- Product differences
- Brand identity
- Impact on quality/performance
- Buyer profits
- Decision makers' incentives

Determinants of substitution threat

- Relative price performance of substitutes
- Switching costs
- Buyer propensity to substitute

Threat of new entrants

Bargaining power of suppliers

Bargaining power of Buyers

Threat of substitutes

Intensity of Rivalry

NEW ENTRANTS

SUPPLIERS

INDUSTRY COMPETITORS

BUYERS

SUBSTITUTES

Fig. 10.1 Elements of industry structure

understand two industries: the airline industry and the pharmaceutical industry. Both these industries are undergoing fundamental structural change. The model is used to explain the change, mapping the industry before and after the change. As a way of seeing those industries, the model seems very effective.

PORTER'S CONCLUSION

Porter concludes that to understand an industry it is necessary to identify the five forces that are its essential component parts. These five forces are the intensity of competitive rivalry, buyers, suppliers, the availability of substitutes and the threat of new entrants. Understand those five and their relationship and you have understood the industry. It is the relationship between these five forces which determines whether companies in the industry will have the opportunity to make profits or be forever struggling. Industry Analysis tells us whether this is a good business to be in.

Porter has tested his model in a number of industries. He concludes that it is a useful means of understanding important aspects of any industry. It is a way of mapping what is going on.

The map or model of Industry Analysis allows anyone to understand any industry. By using the model we can predict whether companies in this market will, in general, find profits plentiful and easy to achieve or will, in general, have to fight hard to make any profit.

Furthermore, the model directs our attention to where our strategic advantage or disadvantage lies so that we can do something about it. For example, if the model shows that it is very easy for new competitors to enter our market, we may conclude that when our profits are high new competitors will find it attractive to try to win some of those profits. If, however, we can create barriers to entry we may lessen the threat and so improve our opportunity to make profits. We could do this in a number of ways. We might, for example, lobby government to create trade and tariff barriers to impede foreign competitors. We could differentiate our product so that what we offer is in some way special and unique and not something which would-be new competitors could offer. In effect this is what Coca Cola does with its massive brand advertising. Someone else may want to sell a strange brown liquid. It may taste and smell like Coca Cola. But it is not Coca Cola. So it is unlikely to do much damage to Coca Cola. Only 'Coke is the Real Thing' as they ceaselessly tell us in their adverts. In effect, Coca Cola has erected a high barrier to entry. The only way to win market share from Coca Cola would seem to be to invest equally heavily in creating a rival brand, which is what Pepsi Cola did.

The UK regional electricity utility companies discovered from an analysis of their industry that there is one problem. A supplier, an electricity generating company, has a near monopoly over the supply of electricity which they must buy in order to sell it on to their customers. Having identified their strategic weakness through an industry analysis they overcame it by building their own generator.

A PRE-EXAMINATION OF INDUSTRY ANALYSIS

BEFORE READING THE NEXT SECTION, you are invited to become the examiner assessing Michael Porter's Industry Analysis research. You may find it helpful, as a first step, to identify

- the research question
- the conclusion
- the logic that leads from question to conclusion.

You can then set about examining the steps in the logic.

EXAMINING INDUSTRY ANALYSIS

WHAT IS THE RESEARCH QUESTION?

In the research which resulted in Porter's Industry Analysis the focal question was: 'What is it that makes an industry attractive or unattractive?'

That same question could have been put differently, as for example: 'Is it possible to map the key factors that drive an industry and determine its relative profitability and attractiveness?'

WHAT IS THE RESEARCH CONCLUSION?

Here is a model, a means of mapping any industry, which will tell us whether this is a good business to be in. And why. And what to do about it.

WHAT ARE THE STEPS IN THE RESEARCH LOGIC THAT LEAD FROM RESEARCH QUESTION TO CONCLUSION?

1. Here is a theoretical model of how we think any industry should work, based on economic theory and on game theory.
2. We have tested it on several industries.
3. We believe it will work with any industry.

EXAMINE THE LOGIC

Logic Step 1. The theoretical model

All of Porter's work, both Industry Analysis and Generic Strategies, is heavily based on theoretical argument. It is deductive reasoning. He imagines what an industry should be, then goes into the field to check his model against reality. Thus, to examine Porter's model we should first examine his theoretical foundations. They are based on economics. Consequently, Porter's model deals only with economic factors – for example, with demand and supply competing against one another.

The model concentrates on competition. The aim of strategy is taken to be: to achieve a better competitive position than the other players. This makes the model less applicable where cooperation between a company and its customer or supplier is an important strategy. In game theory terms the model assumes **win-lose**; in striking a deal with a supplier the more profit the supplier gains from the deal the less profit the company makes. That may usually be true, but it does not include the possibility of a cooperative agreement to the mutual advantage of both parties, a practice becoming more common in the oil industry, for example.

The Industry Analysis model is also based on the assumption that the important factors in strategy are competition and securing a competitive advantage. While this may be important, the model leaves out anything else. Models are, by definition, simplifications of reality. Simply following Porter's model does not guarantee that a company will have a successful strategy. At best it will be successful in the areas that Porter's model treats.

Logic Step 2. We have tested it on several industries

The questions the examiners will ask are:

- Has the model been adequately tested?
- Can we rely on it to be equally relevant to all industries or to some more limited range of application?

Has Porter really subjected the model to the most rigorous possible tests, or has he simply selected those industries best suited to demonstrating his model? Here we are on familiar territory: the need to be rigorously objective about destruction testing our own pet theories, the role of research methodology to prevent us misleading ourselves.

Before relying on the model, practitioners will test it carefully to see whether it really does apply to their industry. Some who have tested it report some difficulties.

Logic Step 3. We believe it will work on any industry

- Has it been tested on a very wide range of industries?
- Has it been tested by independent researchers and do they obtain the same results?

These are the familiar questions of **generalizability** and **reproducibility** which we discussed earlier.

If Porter was a research student he would expect to be closely questioned on these points by his examiners. Since he is a professor and leading authority on strategy, his ideas have been very thoroughly examined, debated, and argued over in the press and in seminar rooms. Porter, being a wily fellow, doubtless subjected his own research to the most rigorous examination before publishing it. You can always be sure that someone is intending to give you a hard time. So you need to examine your own work to identify its weaknesses before they do, and while you still have time to remedy them properly. That does not mean seek to conceal them.

Now let us examine Porter's second big idea, Generic Strategies.

GENERIC STRATEGIES

Porter's second question is: 'How does a company achieve a position of relative competitive advantage in its industry?'

Porter's proposal is that there are only two ways in which a company can compete: do it better or do it cheaper. In Porter's terminology that is **differentiation** or **cost advantage**. The customer must be offered a product or service with some significant advantage over competing products. Or, if it is no better than its competitors, then the only way it will win the sale is by offering a lower price.

The model for Generic Strategies is shown in Fig. 10.2.

Having established a clear and simple model, Porter again provides the empirical evidence on video. He offers the example of Ivory Soap from Procter & Gamble. Ivory competes on being lower priced than its competitors, 'a good basic soap at a realistic price'. The Ivory example makes the point that low-cost products still have to offer acceptable quality. High-quality differentiated products still have to be sold at a price the customer will pay. Porter offers the example of La Quinta Inns, hotels in the southern states of the USA that cater for a carefully defined target customer, who does not want room service or a bar. Porter's work tends to be familiar to students of management. It also leaves some students feeling uneasy. Some of the reasons for that uneasiness become apparent when we subject Porter to critical examination.

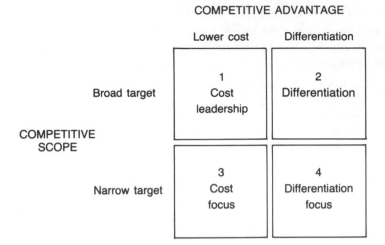

Fig. 10.2 Porter's Generic Strategies

A PRE-EXAMINATION OF GENERIC STRATEGIES

Porter proposes that the competitive strategy of all companies should henceforth be conducted in accordance with his model. This, says Porter, is how to do strategy.

That bold statement demands very thorough and rigorous testing. As a final practice, decide how you would put Porter and his theory to the test. You may put yourself in the role of Porter's external examiner. Or you may be a company manager considering whether this is the way you should run your company. Or you may choose to put yourself in the shoes of Michael Porter wishing to check his ideas very carefully before going public, knowing that such a bold claim will attract the most rigorous and noisy examination.

To examine Porter's research one can usefully begin, as we did with Peters and Waterman's research, by pinpointing

- the research question
- the research conclusion
- the research logic which leads from question to conclusion.

That will take us immediately to the heart of Porter's research.

Equally important is to apply the tests of theory and knowledge which we discussed earlier, such as

Empirical testing

Does it work in practice? Has it been sufficiently tested in field trials? Has the researcher set out to destruction test his pet theory? The need for impartiality, for **non-attachment** is especially relevant here where Porter is generating a theory from first principles and then going out to find examples which test it rigorously. Or are they examples chosen to support the theory? Porter is as human as we are when it comes to favouring our own pet ideas and theories.

Logical consistency, credibility

Do we believe it? If not, why not? Does the theory seem logical?

The interplay of theory and data

Do the facts speak for themselves? They seldom do. Most often we as researchers have to make some sense of a pile of facts. In effect we supply the meaning, the theory which connects a series of otherwise unconnected data or observations.

The important question to ask of any researcher, Porter included, is: 'Does the interplay of objective evidence and subjective interpretation give us something, some new knowledge, which we are prepared to rely upon, at least until something better comes along?' Remember the quote from C. G. Jung:

> Nowhere is the basic requirement so indispensable that the observer should be adequate to his object, in the sense of being able to see not only subjectively but also objectively. The demand that he should see only objectively is quite out of the question, for it is impossible. We must be satisfied if he does not see too subjectively.
>
> (Jung, 1971)

Does Porter convince you? His research is presented in his books, *Competitive Strategy* and *Competitive Advantage* and on video, which are well known to many readers. How well does Porter's published work stand up to the tests of validity which we discussed in the early chapters on research methodology?

BEFORE READING THE NEXT SECTION, use what you have learned so far to help you examine Porter's research, as a prelude to examining your own. With practice you can become a better examiner of your own research than the external examiners. Then you have the means of creating successful research.

EXAMINING GENERIC STRATEGIES

Porter's research method throughout appears to be to develop a model by logical deduction drawing on related academic traditions, then go out and test it empirically in the field. Watching the videos and reading Porter's books one sometimes feels that the examples given are chosen to demonstrate Porter's theory rather than to test it. It may be that at an earlier stage Porter went diligently through the essential process of destruction testing his theory, seeking empirical evidence and examples that would prove his theory wrong and send him in search of a better explanation. Unless the reader sees the full test he or she cannot be wholly convinced.

A second concern is that if one were to observe Porter's examples of La Quinta and Ivory Soap without any prior knowledge of Porter's theories, one might not see in them what Porter sees. La Quinta is presented as having identified precisely what the target customer wants and provided it exactly. The innocent reader might take that to be a fine example of differentiation. La Quinta is meeting that customer's needs better than any other hotel does. But Porter intends La Quinta as an example of competing on lowest cost. Here we have an example of that well-known phenomenon, Northrop's Martian.

> Northrop asks us to imagine a Martian visitor, assumed to be quite intelligent but unacquainted with theoretical developments in modern physics, observing a Wilson cloud-chamber experiment. He is quite capable of noting all the operations, all the pointer readings being available to him. But what, asks Northrop, would this experiment prove to him about the existence of electrons? Northrop concludes that without the aids of concepts defined theoretically (nonoperationally) our Martian friend would learn nothing about electrons. The implication is clearly that something in addition to operational definitions is necessary.
>
> (Blalock, 1968)

Northrop's Martian would be a helpful visitor in the psychology laboratory. Observing the experiment where a rat learns to press a button which rings a bell to obtain food, who would our Martian conclude had trained whom? Has the professor trained the rat to press the bell in order to get food? Or has the rat trained the professor to bring food whenever the rat rings for it? And if the Martian happened to have four legs, a tail, and a pointy face, would that affect his judgement?

Porter's concepts and models allow managers to look at industries and competitive strategies in a novel way. Their usefulness seems to rest not so much in giving us an exact definition of the way an industry is, but more in giving an analytical tool for understanding industries, and certain aspects of companies. That in itself is valuable, as many companies have realized. Porter's work on generic strategies may be more useful if one does not view him as saying there are two strategies: differentiation and low cost. It may be more beneficial to use the model to re-examine our own company's competitive strategy, decide what precisely we offer to which precise target customer, what combination of price and special qualities, make sure that we all know what we are doing, and test how well we actually deliver on our promises.

Research that gives us an analytical device which helps us see more clearly can be very worthwhile.

TESTS OF VALIDITY

The Porter research and the Peters and Waterman project present an interesting problem for us. How do we know that what they have concluded is reliable? Peters and Waterman have expounded eight cardinal principles for successful enterprises. If they are right, companies should follow these eight principles to become successful. Porter proposes two models with accompanying theories with which companies can create for themselves more effective competitive strategies. Are they right? How do we know? How can we test the theories and recommendations of Porter, of Peters and Waterman, and of others like them to discover whether they really do give us better ways of managing companies? The test is urgently needed. More theorists will follow in the footsteps of Porter, and of Peters and Waterman, each inventing new ways to save the corporate world, new recipes for success and profits. The shelves of every airport bookshop, and every business bookshop, are full of titles and gurus purporting to tell managers how to make money and how to do their jobs. Titles abound on such topics as 'How to be a better manager in just one minute a day'; 'How to thrive on disorder and disaster'; 'Creative use of chaos and cock-up'; 'The five-minute MBA course'; 'The management secrets of Genghis Khan'. Some of these may contain a grain of truth. Some may be nonsense, or dangerous if taken internally. How can we separate the wheat from the chaff?

EMPIRICAL TESTING: DOES IT WORK IN PRACTICE?

Before we test the ideas on our own business we want to see the author's evidence that his or her ideas have worked in many other businesses. If the businesses quoted by the author are successful we still want to know if they succeeded because of his or her advice, not in spite of it. Just because it worked in a few examples chosen by the author does not mean that it is bound to work in our company. We want to know if the theory is generally valid, if it is relevant to our business, which is the test of **generalizability** which we saw earlier. Most important, we want to assess the quality and extent of the author's **empirical testing**. Has the theory been tested against an extensive and exhaustive range of examples? Or has the author just chosen examples which conveniently will support his or her ideas? Has the author really objectively and dispassionately gone out and searched for examples where the theory does not work? If not, and if we are not convinced that the author has, then we will treat the ideas with appropriate suspicion, and not bet our whole business on them. They may, nonetheless, give us some useful ideas which we can explore for ourselves. Perhaps we can make something out of them.

INTERNAL LOGICAL CONSISTENCY

The author proposes a model of the world. Does it seem logical, or credible? It does not seek to capture the whole world, but it does claim to be a useful true model of a part of the real world. Are the elements of the model consistent with one another? Does the model adequately explain the evidence? Some reviewers have worried over this aspect of Porter's theory. They worry about whether it is logical to leave out Government and the State from the list of forces that determine the profitability of an industry. They worry, too, about whether it is helpful to say that there are only two broad types of strategy available, differentiation and cost. Are there not other ways to present a better deal to the customer? Is there an implication in the model that it is either-or: either cost advantage or differentiation? Can it not be both together?

The test of **internal logical consistency** is to take the author's theory and examine whether it seems logical; whether the parts fit together harmoniously; whether there are any internal inconsistencies.

RANGE OF COVERAGE

Any model is a simplification of the real world. It deals with a limited range of situations, and only with a few aspects of those situations. A model is useful precisely because it picks out a few key elements and the relationship between them. It leaves out far more than it includes.

To assess the worth of a model or theory we must be clear about what it covers and what it does not cover, where it is relevant and where it is not. No model can be all things to all people. For example Porter's models are concerned with competitive positioning. They do not fit easily with the present state of the public sector National Health Service in Britain, though they can be used to give an impression of what the NHS might become. Peters and Waterman's eight principles are concerned with excellence. They are derived from excellent companies. They are not directly concerned with under-achievers, nor why they under-achieve, nor how to turn them round. Managers in a company or a university that does not have a bias for action may wish they had such a bias, but not know how to get one. *In Search of Excellence* aims to show why successful companies are successful. It does not set out to be a manual of how to transform a failing or mediocre organization, nor one that is adequate but less than excellent. That is outside its *range of coverage*.

Understanding the range of coverage of a new theory or model is important because it tells us whether it applies to our company.

Many of the validity tests which we saw earlier, such as *verisimilitude* and *congruence with existing theory*, apply equally powerfully to the work of Porter, and of Peters and Waterman. They help us to put the new ideas in perspective, to assess how good they are, and what they are good for.

DECONSTRUCTION OF UNDERLYING ANALOGY

New models and theories usually work by pointing out similarities between the new unknown situation and older familiar situations.

We do not know how to gain an advantage over the other forces competing for supremacy in our industry. In some respects, however, this resembles armies competing for superiority on the battlefield, and we **do know** about that. We have a body of knowledge, a set of theories, techniques, and established practice about warfare, about competing on the battlefield. Perhaps we can apply these to the problem of competing in markets and industries.

The underlying analogy is both the strength and the weakness of the new theory. It gives us a way of dealing with the new situation so that it is no longer wholly unknown. We have a means of understanding it and dealing with it through the knowledge we already have of a familiar, analogous situation. But the analogy carries certain weaknesses. True, armies compete in battle, companies compete in markets; in that they are alike. But companies can also cooperate in markets. The analogy does not hold good in that respect. That imparts a weakness and a limitation to the model. The analogy can take us part of the way towards understanding the new situation, but not all the way. The new situation is like the old in some respects. But the new situation is not the old. Markets may resemble battlefields in some respects, but they are not battlefields. It is not usual to seek to kill the commander of the opposing company, for example.

The debate over Porter's theory still continues. That is a testimony to the importance of what he proposes – a new and all-embracing theory of strategy. Many companies are adopting Porter's theory and using it. Many others are sceptical. An MBA student at City University, London, recently said to me, 'I've just realized why it is that I have always felt uneasy about Porter. It's because he's an economist.' If I have understood him correctly the student was raising concerns about inductive and deductive logic, about the interplay of theory and data, about the need for rigorous empirical testing and, above all, about the need for common sense.

Now, for the pleasure of watching a master craftsman at work, let us look at Geert Hofstede's work on understanding culture.

Culture's Consequences   11

For any company operating across national borders the difficulties of dealing with different cultures is a daily experience. In a recent experience of my own, a French organization and a British organization were seeking to develop a relationship which might lead to a joint venture, at least to cooperation. The approaches of the two nationalities to building the relationship were quite different. Worse, they were mutually incomprehensible. Worse still, they each misinterpreted the other side's behaviour and motives so that the relationship nearly died. When the British team went to Paris they were entertained to several excellent meals, good food, good wine, good hospitality. They were given a private guided tour of one of France's best museums of the French culture. The museum was open only for them. After two such meetings the British were beginning to suspect that the French were not serious. 'They don't seem to want to get down to business.' 'They avoid discussing anything concrete.' 'They don't want to be tied down to anything specific.' 'It's all talk and no substance.' (The actual phrase used was less polite.)

The third meeting was on British soil. The British tried to organize the meeting in the way which they thought appropriate to a serious business meeting. There was a formal agenda, a chairman, the purpose of the meeting was to reach a formal agreement which would be committed to written form and be a legally binding contract. Privately, the French thought this rather offensive. There is no trust, no relationship. They only want to have penalty clauses and lawyers.

Each side saw its own behaviour as perfectly comprehensible, appropriate, and the best way to ensure a good relationship. Each side found the other side's behaviour inappropriate, not conducive to a good relationship. They were interpreting the foreigners' behaviour as they would if one of their own compatriots behaved in that way. The British behaved as they would if a Briton avoided all contractual commitments, refused to be bound to anything, objected to any talk of penalties for non-performance. Such a Briton would not be taken seriously as a would-be partner in a joint venture. The French had sought to establish a social relationship first on the assumption that friendship, once established, would lead to a firm basis for business. The British reaction was interpreted in the way that a similar reaction from a Frenchman would be interpreted. A Frenchman who did not respond to hospitality, repulsed attempts at friendship, seemed impatient with the culture of his hosts and who was concerned only to have his lawyers tie them up in knots and punishments would be viewed as barbaric, unsympathetic, not our kind of people.

Polite convention prevented either side from voicing these perceptions to each other. The joint venture was only saved by a small number of participants who happened to have experience of both cultures and understood what was happening.

It is this situation of cultural differences that Hofstede has chosen to explore.

RESEARCH OBJECTIVES

Hofstede had been exposed to cultural differences for a number of years before embarking on the formal research into *Culture's Consequences*.

> The research project has a long history, going back to the first international HERMES survey. I could not foresee then that my involvement with this survey should eventually lead to my spending five years on in-depth research on culture's consequences. Some of us suspected the scientific importance of HERMES data. My colleagues went off on to other tasks; I alone remained to follow the intellectual track.

The importance and value of the study was clear to Hofstede. The **added value** of the project, the contribution which the project would, if successful, make to a wider audience was clear.

> The survival of mankind will depend to a large extent on the ability of people who think differently to act together. International collaboration presupposes some understanding of where other people's thinking differs from ours. Exploring the way in which nationality predisposes our thinking is therefore not an intellectual luxury. A better understanding of invisible cultural differences is one of the main contributions the social sciences can make to practical policy makers in governments, organisations and institutions – and to ordinary citizens.

The questions at the design stage of any research – while the researcher is still writing the project plan – are:

- Will the output justify the input?
- Will the results of the project justify all the time and effort which it will consume?

Hofstede, at the start of his project, believes it will. That belief in the value of the project is necessary to drive the researcher on throughout the life of the project.

It led me from psychology into sociology and then into political science and anthropology. It led us to living as a family in three countries, while surviving on money from five. To a large extent it determined our lives over the past eight years. It was not always smooth and easy, but we have not regretted it. Never a dull moment.

The project's objective was to identify and to understand what culture is, and how it leads to cultural differences in thinking and values.

This research explores the differences in thinking and social action that exist between members of 40 different modern nations. . . .
    Cross-cultural studies proliferate in all the social sciences, but they usually lack a theory of the key variable, culture itself. Names of countries are usually treated as residues of undefined variance in the phenomena found. The research aims at being specific about the elements of which culture is composed.

Hofstede does not begin the research with a mind like a blank sheet of paper ready for the data to write upon it. He has some ideas already. He believes that there is such a thing as culture. And cultural differences. And that they can be identified and grasped.

It argues that people carry mental programs which are developed in the family in early childhood and reinforced in schools and organisations, and that these mental programs contain a component of national culture. They are most clearly expressed in the different values that predominate among people from different countries.

Hofstede had also seen and mused upon the results of the HERMES survey of cultural differences among managers of different nationalities working for one large multi-national company. It was the feeling that this survey data pointed to something important that helped to set him off on the research trail.

RESEARCH METHODS

Hofstede had access to a huge data base. A survey, held twice, of 116 000 managers in forty countries working for subsidiaries of one multi-national corporation. All 116 000 managers completed a question-naire 'covering among other things questions about values'.

This data base was supplemented by additional data collected from a similar survey of managers of many nationalities attending courses at IMEDE Business School in Switzerland.

Hofstede compared his results with thirty-eight other studies by dif-ferent authors, indicating that he took the tests of *intersubjectivity, rep-etition*, and *theoretical congruence* very seriously indeed. (For which, see Chapter 5.)

In designing the research Hofstede has two major methodological problems:

1. How to discover people's cultural attitudes. (He tackles this problem by asking them multi-choice questions in a questionnaire.)
2. How to make sense of the responses.

The responses allow Hofstede to conclude that so many managers answer question 1 by circling number 1. The first question is:

How important is it to: 1. Have sufficient time left for your personal or family life?

   1   of utmost importance
   2   very important
   3   of moderate importance
   4   of little importance
   5   of very little or no importance.

An example of the questions which Hofstede uses to discover the cul-ture and values of respondents can be seen in Fig. 11.1.

Analysis of the data also allows the researcher to discover whether there is a significant correlation between the answers to this question and the nationality of the respondents. Further analysis allows a com-parison between nationalities. Do Italians, for example, attach more importance than the Japanese to family life?

Yet further analysis can discover whether there is a consistent pattern in the answers to several questions. Does a particular nationality give high importance to family life and to low job stress and to opportunity for high savings, for example? All of these correlations can be dis-covered from a detailed statistical analysis of the responses. He has a very large number of responses to work with.

At some point Hofstede has to go beyond the data and supply a construct. WHY do managers of a certain nationality consistently give

VALUES SURVEY MODULE
(RECOMMENDED FOR FUTURE
CROSS-CULTURAL SURVEY STUDIES)

Please think of an ideal job – disregarding your present job. In choosing an ideal job, how important would it be to you to (please circle one answer number in each line across):

	of utmost importance	very important	of moderate importance	of little importance	of very little or no importance
1. Have sufficient time left for your personal or family life?	1	2	3	4	5
2. Have challenging tasks to do, from which you can get a personal sense of accomplishment?	1	2	3	4	5
3. Have little tension and stress on the job?	1	2	3	4	5
4. Have good physical working conditions (good ventilation and lighting, adequate work space, etc.)?	1	2	3	4	5
5. Have good working relationship with your direct superior?	1	2	3	4	5
6. Have security of employment?	1	2	3	4	5
7. Have considerable freedom to adopt your own approach to the job?	1	2	3	4	5
8. Work with people who cooperate well with one another?	1	2	3	4	5
9. Be consulted by your direct superior in his/her decisions?	1	2	3	4	5
10. Make a real contribution to the success of your company or organization?	1	2	3	4	5
11. Have an opportunity for high earnings?	1	2	3	4	5
12. Serve your country?	1	2	3	4	5

Fig. 11.1 An example of Hofstede's questions.

higher scores to certain questions than do managers of another nationality? What is the reason for the differences in the responses? The data may be very extensive but it does not interpret itself. The data may show that Dutch managers give high scores to questions 1, 17, 28, 34, 82. German managers give lower scores to these and higher scores to other questions. But the data does not tell us WHY. We still need a key to unlock the mystery, to explain WHY respondents prefer to tick the boxes that they do. The key is a **concept** which helps us to understand the reasons why managers of a particular nationality answer as they do. The concept comes not from the data but from the researcher who supplies it as a means of understanding the data. Here again we have the interplay of data and concept, of objective and subjective, the 'hunches that have arisen from the interplay between me and my material'.

RESEARCH CONCLUSIONS

Hofstede concludes that the cultural differences of countries can best be understood on four dimensions.

> The four dimensions on which country cultures differ were revealed by theoretical reasoning and statistical analysis.

The four dimensions are

- Power distance
- Uncertainty avoidance
- Individualism
- Masculinity.

> Each of the 40 countries could be given a score on these four dimensions. . . . The same four dimensions are reflected in data from completely different sources, both survey studies of various kinds and non-survey comparative studies. Altogether data from 38 other studies comparing from 5 to 39 countries are significantly correlated with one or more of the four dimensions.

Itself a useful test of validity.

As an example of Hofstede's concepts or dimensions let us consider **power distance**.

> The first of the four dimensions of national culture which the HERMES data reveal is called Power Distance. The basic issue involved, to which different societies have found different solutions, is human inequality. . . . This inequality is usually formalised in

hierarchical boss-subordinate relationships. . . . These questions deal with perceptions of the superior's style of decision-making and of colleagues' fear to disagree with superiors, and with the type of decision-making which subordinates prefer in their boss . . .

I chose as the central questionnaire item for exploring power differences between countries,

> How frequently in your experience does the following problem occur:
>> employees being afraid to express disagreement with their managers?

with a five point answer scale from 'very frequently' to 'very seldom'.

Two other questions are used to give information on power distance in boss-subordinate relationships.

The descriptions below apply to four different types of managers. First, please read through these descriptions:

Manager 1   Usually makes his/her decisions promptly and communicates them to his/her subordinates clearly and firmly. Expects them to carry out the decisions loyally and without raising difficulties.

Manager 2   Usually makes his/her decisions promptly, but, before going ahead, tries to explain them fully to his/her subordinates. Gives them the reasons for the decisions and answers whatever questions they may have.

Manager 3   Usually consults with his/her subordinates before he/she reaches his/her decisions. Listens to their advice, considers it, and then announces his/her decision. He/she then expects all to work loyally to implement it whether or not it is in accordance with the advice they gave.

Manager 4   Usually calls a meeting of his/her subordinates when
(version   there is an important decision to be made. Puts the prob-
1967–   lem before the group and invites discussion. Accepts the
1969)   majority viewpoint as the decision.

             Usually calls a meeting of his/her subordinates when
(version   there is an important decision to be made. Puts the prob-
1970–   lem before the group and tries to obtain consensus. If
1973)   he/she obtains consensus, he/she accepts this as the
             decision. If consensus is impossible, he/she usually
             makes the decision him/herself.

A54 Now for the above types of manager, please mark the *one* which you would prefer to work under.
1. Manager 1
2. Manager 2
3. Manager 3
4. Manager 4

A55 And, to which *one* of the above four types of managers would you say your own manager *most closely corresponds*?
1. Manager 1
2. Manager 2
3. Manager 3
4. Manager 4
5. He does not correspond closely to any of them.

Table 11.1 Power Distance Index (PDI) Values by country based on the scores on three attitude survey questions for a stratified sample of seven occupations at two points in time

Country	PDI Actual	PDI Predicted	Country	PDI Actual	PDI Predicted
Philippines	94	73	USA	40	42
Mexico	81	70	Canada	39	36
Venezuela	81	66	Netherlands	38	38
India	77	78	Australia	36	44
Singapore	74	64	Germany (F.R.)	35	42
Brazil	69	72	Great Britain	35	45
Hong Kong	68	56	Switzerland	34	32
France	68	42	Finland	33	30
Colombia	67	75	Norway	31	27
Turkey	66	60	Sweden	31	23
Belgium	65	36	Ireland	28	37
Peru	64	69	New Zealand	22	35
Thailand	64	74	Denmark	18	28
Chile	63	56	Israel	13	44
Portugal	63	53	Austria	11	40
Greece	60	51			
Iran	58	61			
Taiwan	58	63	Mean of 39 countries (HERMES)	51	52
Spain	57	56			
Pakistan	55	74			
Japan	54	57			
Italy	50	53	Yugoslavia (same industry)	76	53
South Africa	49	62			
Argentina	49	56			

Actual values and values predicted on the basis of multiple regression on latitude, population size, and wealth.

The countries in which highest Power Distance Index scores are recorded, where the cultural norm is for subordinates to be most afraid to disagree with the boss, are Philippines, Mexico, Venezuela, India. Those most unafraid to disagree with the boss are Austrians, Israelis, Danes, New Zealanders, Irish. The full list is shown in Table 11.1.

Our purpose here is not to summarize the whole of Hofstede's research but to show how it works. Hofstede knows what he is interested in: cultural differences and their consequences. To observe these differences he uses a survey questionnaire to a very large number of managers, 116 000 in forty countries. From their responses to multiple-choice questions analysed statistically he identifies patterns and correlations. These he takes to be evidence of cultural differences. He then has to discover what are these cultural differences of which the responses are evidence. He suggests four concepts, or dimensions as he calls them, which explain cultural difference. He connects particular questions from the survey to each of the four dimensions, e.g. questions A54, A55, B46 show the respondents' feelings about power distance. Finally, he plots each country's position on each of the four dimensions as a means of identifying and explaining the culture of that country.

A PRE-EXAMINATION OF *CULTURE'S CONSEQUENCES*

At this point you, as reader, are asked to form your own judgement of Hofstede's research.

- Is it reliable?
- Do you believe it?
- How do you know?

More generally, what tests are appropriate to assess the validity of research such as this?

Resist the temptation to read the next section. You need to have the ability to identify appropriate tests of the validity of your own research before the examiners do. Throughout your management career you will be offered many new management theories, recipes and quick fixes. You will need skill in deciding which are worthwhile and which are hogwash.

Use Hofstede's research as a practice run.

EXAMINING *CULTURE'S CONSEQUENCES*

How do we decide whether Hofstede's conclusions are valid, reliable, trustworthy?

Before we use it to help us manage our dealings with foreign people we need to feel safe that it will not make matters worse. We do not want it to lead us into making a major *faux pas* thinking that we know what we are doing. How can we be sure that the Hofstede four-dimensions theory delivers everything that it promises?

There are several ways of checking.

We have our own experience of dealing with strange foreign cultures and natives. Does what Hofstede says match our experience? Does it explain the problems of the Anglo-French joint venture, and of David in Thailand, cited earlier? MBA classes tend to be extremely multinational. Does Hofstede help to explain their experience? Does his theory fit their empirical experience? For myself I found Hofstede's work very valuable in making sense of various intercultural experiences and misunderstandings accumulated over many years in many countries. This test involves **intersubjectivity**, i.e. Hofstede can see the four dimensions at work explaining intercultural experience. So can I. So can other people.

We can compare Hofstede's conclusions with other research in the same subject area. Hofstede, being a good researcher, has already done this. But we shall do it ourselves if we are to test the research and not take it on trust. This is the test of **theoretical convergence**. Other people's theories lead to the same conclusion.

We can do some **empirical testing** by carrying out our own survey of people from different cultures. Hofstede has provided his questionnaires in appendices to his report. We can use them to conduct our own survey with our own sample of foreign managers to see if we get the same results, whether in fact the research is **repeatable**.

Hofstede's research was based largely on the data drawn from 116 000 managers from ONE multi-national company. Do the results apply with equal validity to all other companies, or was there something special about Hofstede's company that biased the results? In other words is it **generalizable**? This we can discover by conducting the survey in other companies. Remember that Peters and Waterman took great pains to ensure that their sixty-three companies were drawn from a wide range of industries and technologies so that they could reasonably be said to be *representative* of American companies in general. Interestingly, applying Hofstede's findings to Peters and Waterman's research does raise the question of whether their principles are only valid for American companies since that is where the bulk of their evidence comes from. The best way to manage a company may depend on national culture. What works in the USA may not always work in France, India, Holland, or elsewhere.

How reliable is Hofstede as a research instrument? Where is he coming from? What are his biases? Why does he interpret the data in the way he does? Hofstede to his credit has foreseen this test. He gives an appendix to his report explaining his own cultural heritage. This allows us to weigh up for ourselves Hofstede's perceptual biases in arriving at his concepts and theories. It also indicates a strong degree of *self-awareness* on his part in conducting the research.

Research into values cannot be value-free. In fact few human activities can be value-free. This book reflects not only the values of HERMES employees and IMEDE course participants, but between the lines the values of the author. It will I hope be read by readers with a variety of different values. In this Appendix I try as best I can to be explicit about my own value system.

Hofstede then explains how he would answer his own questionnaire, and explains his own conceptual values that this reveals. He explains, too, his background which formed his culture.

The origins of my value system, like everyone else's are found in my national background, social class and family roots, education, and life experience. . . . I was born in the Netherlands and lived there (for more than forty years). . . . I completed a university education in the Netherlands. . . . We lived through the German occupation (1940–45) without physical suffering but detesting the occupants. I was too young at the time to understand the full scope of the ethical issues involved in Nazism, but I had seen my Jewish schoolmates being deported never to return. Only in the years after 1945 did I fully realise that for five years we had lived under a system in which everything I held for white was called black and vice versa, which made me more conscious of what were my values, and that it is sometimes necessary to take explicit positions.

We should also examine Hofstede's *questionnaire design* to see whether it is reliable and unbiased; to see whether it is capable of measuring what it claims to measure. We can examine the **sample size and selection** to test whether it is sufficiently large and unbiased as to be a representative sample of the world at large. We can examine his **statistical analysis** to test whether the correlations which he sees in his thousands of responses are reliably there.

We should also test whether the jump from the data to the concepts is reasonable and acceptable: that is, does it have *verisimilitude*. This is the subjective area of the interplay of theory and data, 'the relationship between me and my material', of which we spoke earlier. This is a subjective area where we can only exercise our personal judgement and that of colleagues. If we are considering using the theory, do we ourselves trust the research? Do we consider that the concepts can reasonably be read into the data?

But the personal equation asserts itself even more in the presentation and communication of one's own observations, to say nothing of the interpretation and abstract exposition of the empirical material. . . . The demand that he should see only objectively is quite out of the question, for it is impossible. We must be satisfied if he does not see too subjectively.

(Jung, 1971)

In conclusion, it is possible to test very thoroughly the validity of Hofstede's theory. Having completed the tests, we can then decide whether we shall use it.

PART FOUR
Reporting the Research

Managing the data   **12**

The research accumulates a great mound of paper. To this are added impressions, thoughts, and ideas. The great mound of data has to be organized, managed, and controlled. New data from interviews have to be captured, recorded, and retained for later use. Relevant quotes from books and articles have to be remembered, retained, and accessible. A research project requires a thoroughly organized system of data management.

The following tips on how to shepherd the unruly data have been gathered from other researchers and from experience.

THE PROJECT PLAN

The project plan is an essential part of the first stage of every project (see Chapter 1). Part of its function is to plan in advance precisely what information we need, where it is, how we will get it, and when. Throughout the progress of the project we shall be referring back to the project plan to check that we are on course for successful completion by the due date. When we drift off course or fall behind schedule, a regular check on the project plan will immediately reveal the discrepancy so that we can take remedial action the moment it is needed. The plan will not be perfect first time. It can be improved and amended in the light of new knowledge as we proceed.

INTERNAL AND EXTERNAL MEMORIES

You have the internal memory capacity of your own brain. You will need to supplement this with an external memory. Write it all down on paper, or store it on computer disk if that is your preferred external memory. Every interview must be written up thoroughly on paper or disk **before** the next interview begins. A photocopy of every important passage in a book must be retained, with the key points underlined.

Each must be supplemented by a written note of the ideas, thoughts, and reflections you had about them at the time. Full cross-referencing information is essential on each written record giving data, place, people involved, book title and author, where kept, and so on as appropriate. When you eventually write your report that particular piece of information may be vital. You must be able to lay your hand on it immediately. The anguished sighing of 'Oh, where did I see that piece of data' has a wonderful capacity for ruining your train of thought.

The pages of notes need to be organized as they are collected. One way of doing it is to have a separate file for each chapter of the final report. A file each for

- the brief;
- the introduction explaining the objectives, purpose, and methods of the project;
- the literature, i.e. what has already been written on the subject;
- the research methodology;
- the data:
  (a) interview reports;
  (b) survey data;
  (c) other data;
- the analysis of the data;
- bibliography and references.

All of these are being accumulated as the research progresses. Other essential chapters, such as the executive summary, conclusions, recommendations, index, etc., are written towards the end of the research period. Keeping the accumulating data in files for each chapter of the final report keeps the data under control and easily accessible. It also makes the final write-up much easier.

THOUGHTS DIARY

You may find it helpful to keep a notebook with you at all times to jot down flashes of insight that may pop into your mind. Colin Eden of Strathclyde University in Scotland always keeps a hardback notebook with him 'in case I have an idea'. The mind seems to work well 'off-line' as it were. You may not be consciously concentrating on your research at all, when into your head comes an idea, an insight which illuminates everything. Or a connection between separate bits of data suddenly occurs to you. It can happen when you are on a train, in the bath, or digging the garden, or at any time when you do not expect it. It does sometimes seem that the rational, linear-working left-hand part of the brain is good for organized routine tasks like analysing data, doing statistics, analysing questionnaires, writing up notes. And another non-linear, non-routine, non-organized part of the brain pro-vides flashes of insights, inspirations, connections. These flashes are brilliant and sparkling when they happen but they are soon gone. So write them down fully immediately. They have to be written down fully, otherwise the routine, orderly, rational thinking part of the brain will not understand them when it comes to look at them later.

INTERVIEWS

Prepare thoroughly in advance for an interview. Decide why you want the interview, what your objectives are. Decide on your questions. Prepare all of this in writing. Even if it will not be seen in the interview it is an essential *aide-memoire* to you.

Decide how you will structure the interview: how you will allow opportunity for the subject to talk freely and without structured ques-tions; and when you will use structured questions, and what the ques-tions are. Think about how to create a relationship conducive to the interview. Think about what the answers to the questions are likely to be. Often you gain the most telling insights from noticing what the subject avoids telling you, or from the subtle nuances of how it is told.

After the interview, write up the notes in fulsome detail. Write every-thing that comes to mind: how you felt about the interview – your hunches; your impressions about the person and anything of interest at the time. Write it down because it will fade and be lost if you do not. Direct quotations are worth saving because they can bring the final written report to life. Schedule ample writing-up time into the day's work plan. Do the writing-up immediately after each interview and before doing anything else. If that seems too rigid a discipline, try leaving the writing-up until a little later and you will soon discover how much is lost, and how quickly.

PEACE TIME

Set aside time to think, time to dream, time when you deliberately have nothing to do. This can be the most valuable time in your research. This is the time when you can get away from the data and see it in long perspective. Or just have a refreshing rest from it. It is essential not to keep the nose to the grindstone all the time. It induces myopia, tunnel vision and a sore nose.

People who research and consult for a living usually have a special place where they go for undisturbed thinking time. Charles Handy of the London Business School has a cottage in Norfolk where he goes to write. The result is his books, *The Age of Unreason*, *Gods of Management*, and many others. They could not be written in a busy office with

telephone interruptions, smouldering in-trays, and visitors from Por-
lock. Stafford Beer, cybernetician, consultant and author keeps a
secluded cottage in a quarry in north Wales where he goes to think,
write, and meditate. This book is being written in a log cabin in the
woods far from telephones and interruptions, which my kids call 'Dad's
Wendy House'. The important point is to have a sanctuary. Somewhere
you can go to be free, to escape interruptions. To breathe a sigh of
relief and relax. It is in that relaxation that understanding and insight
come in a way that they do not when you are cudgelling your brain
with data, nose to the grindstone, phone in each ear, and the in-tray
on fire. The further you advance in your career the more you will need
the log cabin, or the cottage in Devon, as a sanctuary. When you do,
do not install a telephone. In the meantime you need somewhere quiet,
somewhere that is just as much of a sanctuary. The library of the
university or business school may be the right place for you. Or the
library of another university where no one knows you. Chris Hallibur-
ton, professor at the European School of Management and an international consultant, goes to the RAC Club to write. Some students
doing an MBA part time find it useful to check out of their company
for a week, announcing that they are going to the university. So they
are. Everyone assumes that they are going on a course. In fact they are
getting away from office interruptions so that they can think and do
some real work.

EMOTIONS

Projects have their ups and downs. Projects contain emotional experience. There will be days when you feel brilliant, making progress,
inspired, good. And there will be days when you feel frustrated, perhaps even defeated and getting nowhere. It helps if you know in
advance that these emotions happen and they do not last. The brilliance
passes all too soon. The depression and disgust pass just as quickly if
you let them. The key is not to wallow in them. If the work is not going
well today, if it stinks, if you wish you were not doing this project,
leave it for today. Have a day off. Go and do something you enjoy. Do
not spend your day off feeling guilty for having a day off. You have
awarded yourself a day off for essential remedial purposes. Make the
most of it. Best of all, do something that will take your mind off the
project and off the whole world in which the project exists. Go climb
a mountain. Or slide down a mountain. Go to a concert. Or sail.
Whatever takes you out of yourself. This is a valid, valuable exercise
in itself. Do it thoroughly, with dedication and gusto.

Ninety-nine times out of a hundred the glorious day off is all that is
needed. You return invigorated, all trace of a block vanished. On the

rare occasion of a lasting nagging uncertainty, go get help. Go to the project supervisor. Keep at him or her until you get support – that is what they are there for; use them. Most people get through their projects happily with only the occasional up and down, but it is as well to know how to deal with doldrums.

RITUAL

Ritual can help to get your work flowing. Ritual may be as simple as on-days scheduled for project work, always setting the alarm for a certain time, taking a shower, coffee, then into the library and to work on the project. Without a ritual you could find that you are still in bed. Or having difficulty getting started.

I have a simple reward ritual. I do not have lunch, or the next cup of coffee, until I have reached a pre-designated stopping place, such as the end of a chapter.

When something has gone well, celebrate it. Award yourself a celebration ritual for doing a good job of writing up the methodology, or for mailing that huge pile of questionnaires, or for achieving a particular benchmark on the project plan. Celebration ritual may be going down to the bar for a drink just before it closes. Or a stroll in the park. Or half an hour's sunshine. Whatever. It is a stream of good experiences celebrating good achievements on the research. Be happy. Feel good. The research goes better.

COLLEAGUES

From time to time arrange for colleagues to listen inquiringly while you explain your project to them. You can reciprocate by listening while colleagues explain their research to you. Ask questions. Anything you do not understand, say so. One of the best ways of getting your project clear in your own mind is having to explain it clearly to someone else.

Nearer the time of the presentation and examination your colleagues and you can do a useful service in running practice examination panels for each other. Be sympathetic at first. Then, when you are sufficiently confident, no holds barred.

The written report 13

There comes a time when the research has been done, the data has been collected, the conclusions have been reached, and the researcher knows the answer to the research question. It is now time to **communicate** it. In a very real sense what happens from now on is the most important part of the project.

Consider for a moment what the research and the researcher will be judged on by the target audience.

Q. *What does the client see? What does the client base his or her judgement on?*

A. The written report and the oral presentation.

Q. *What does the academic examining body base its evaluation on?*

A. The written report, the oral presentation, the *viva voce* examination.

When the research work has been done well one has the ingredients for a successful presentation. But remember that these are only the ingredients. What counts is what you do with them.

Consider by way of analogy your favourite restaurant. Earlier in the day the chef has been out to the markets and obtained good ingredients. What matters is what he now does with them. You want to receive an excellent meal, a good experience. You do not want to be presented with a pile of ingredients. Nor do you want to hear a tale of how hard he has had to work in the markets.

This much seems obvious. And yet strangely one does sometimes see inexperienced presenters presenting their audience with piles of ingredients in the raw state, seeking to impress them with how hard they have worked.

There is a tale that a young executive in IBM made this mistake in a presentation to his Board. He was mighty keen to impress them with his effort and application. He reeled out vast amounts of data, facts, observations. The audience was overwhelmed. At the end of the presentation there was silence. The young man's boss and mentor invited him to lunch. The mentor telephoned to reserve a table. Unknown to the young executive he made some special arrangements with the restaurant. When the party arrived for lunch they were seated at their table. Before they could order a waiter arrived and emptied a sack of potatoes in front of them on to the table. To their amazement a second waiter arrived and carefully laid before them a beautiful array of raw sprouts. Finally the chef arrived, welcomed them, sat down at the table and began to recount the exhausting day he had had digging the potatoes. The chef must have overdone the storytelling because the senior executive collapsed in a fit of giggles. Perhaps it was the look of astonishment on the young executive's face as he stared in disbelief at this strange performance. When they had recovered from their laughter they explained to the young man that what the chef had done was precisely what the young executive had done in his presentation. The point was understood and never forgotten. To this day one hears the expression 'a raw potatoes presentation'. They are never made in IBM.

OBJECTIVES

In the pure sciences once the discovery is made it is placed before the scientific community. The results are published in the learned journal appropriate to that subject. The author adopts a pose of indifference. The work is done. The facts are these. How the scientific community will respond is for them to judge. They may take it up and use it if they wish. The play requires that the author, having shown the new fact, remains objective about it, displaying no proprietary interest. Definitely no canvassing.

A business presentation has a different objective. The objective is to make the audience do something. The ideal result of a business presentation is that the audience declares: 'Fine, You've made your case. That's what we'll do.' And they do it.

The entire business presentation is designed to achieve an effect in the minds of the client audience such that they take the desired action. If they take no action the presentation has failed.

Presentation to the academic examiners is also designed to achieve an effect in their minds which leads them to take the desired action.

OUTPUT

There are three main outputs from a management project. The best projects achieve a fourth output. The three main outputs are:

- **The executive summary**
- **The main report**
- **The oral presentation**

The fourth, achieved only in outstanding research, is **publication** in learned and/or professional journals of the findings which make a contribution to knowledge in that subject area.

THE TASK

The researcher has the facts, the evidence, the supporting material, the idea of the solution. Those are the raw materials. The task is to create a change and action on the part of the two client groups.

The vehicle for accomplishing the change is the research report in its three parts: executive summary, main report, oral presentation.

The clients form their judgement on how they will act entirely on the basis of the executive summary, main report, and oral presentation. Nothing else matters now. It does not matter that the researcher has laboured until midnight seven nights and seven days a week for ever. The clients do not see that; they are not interested in that. Those are the researcher's inputs. What matters to the clients are the researcher's outputs. You must have good ingredients. What counts is what you do with them. Now you see why it is that writing-up research, making sense of it and communicating it takes at least as long as all the field-work and data collection. When you have all the data, all the information, all the answers, that completes the first half of the project. The second half of the project, the communication of the results, will determine the class of degree, if any, that is awarded, and whether the client is happy and generous.

Whatever else you may do wrong on your project, do not underestimate the time required and the importance of communicating well the results in the executive summary, the main report, and the oral presentation.

THE EXECUTIVE SUMMARY

The executive summary tells the audience all they need to know in just two pages.

Some busy executives will only read those two pages. Reading the main report may be delegated to someone else. Therefore the executive summary has to be capable of standing alone, making perfectly good sense, and covering everything that is essential for the client audience to know, even if they know nothing else about the research.

Having to communicate the essentials in two pages is an excellent discipline for the researcher. Most researchers have several hundred pages of data and feel that that is the minimum number of pages necessary. Two pages are all you have. Some of your audience will see nothing else. Your recommendations may not be implemented for a year or two, at which time the clients will read the executive summary to refresh their memory. You will not be there to fill in any gaps. The executive summary must contain all the essentials in two pages. It is such a valuable discipline for the researcher that the executive summary should be written before the main report or the preparation for the oral presentation. Once you have created a good executive summary you know what is essential to communicate. You know what the client really needs to know. The essentials obviously vary from one project to another. Here are two sets of questions to get at the essentials of your project. Use either as a structure for your executive summary if you wish.

Example 1: Executive summary

1. The brief. What is the question which this report answers?
2. Why is that important?
3. What did you do? [NB: *Keep this part brief. You only have two pages for the whole executive summary. You can only afford to expend a quarter of a page or thereabouts on this bit.*]
4. What are your essential findings?
5. What do you recommend?
6. What are the costs and benefits of implementing your recommendations?

Example 2: Executive Summary

1. What is the problem? [NB: *You may have to prove simply and powerfully that your client does have a problem. Otherwise it does not need to take any action.*]
2. So what have you found? [*For example: Why do we have a problem? What is the nature of the problem? And the causes?*]
3. What should we do about it?
4. How do we do it?
5. What's in it for us if we do?

Try applying each of these in turn to your own research. They will guide you to the essentials of your own project. Once you have them create the executive summary which best suits your project and gets the right reaction from your audience. Remember: the essential thing is not what you know, but what your client audience needs to know.

There is always a huge amount that you know that your client audience does *not* need to know.

THE MAIN REPORT

Having written the executive summary already has helped you to identify what your clients want from the report, what is essential, and ways of structuring the communication. It is customary to append the executive summary to the front of the main report. **But the main report must be capable of standing alone, making perfectly good clear sense even if nothing else is read or heard.** If some kind soul removes the executive summary as an *aide-memoire* for themselves, the main report has to remain perfectly self-contained without it. Begin again with the design of the main report for an audience who may or may not see the executive summary, who may or may not hear the oral presentation, and who may know nothing whatsoever about you or your work.

There may be some house rules determining how many pages a main report may contain. Usually the house rules allow you plenty of space. The real limiting factor is your audience's attention. Remember that the entire purpose of the report is to get them to get up and do something; to change the world, or some aspect of their organization. They will not do that if you lose their attention, bore them, or bury them under the data heap. Use your material to inspire them to act.

Decide what you want your client groups to do as a result of reading your report. There may be two or three client groups, each needing to do different things.

- Identify clearly the question which this report answers.
- Identify the answer.
- Identify the essential evidence that will lead the audience from question to answer.

Once you have done these things you have planned your main report. The rest is polishing, packaging, topping and tailing.

You probably decided on the structure of your main report and the titles of the chapters at the time you were preparing the project plan. If not here are two models to adapt to suit yourself.

Example 3: The main report

1. Title page
2. The brief
3. Index
4. Introduction: summarizing the whole process to make the report *user*

friendly. No one wants to read to the end to find out what is going on.

5. Main chapters:
   Market
   Competition
   Critical success factors
   Rating own company
   Rating competitors
   Analyses of own company:
       Financial
       Strengths and weaknesses
       Strategy
       Performance
6. Conclusions
   Recommendations
   Appendices.

Example 4: The main report

1. Title page
2. The brief
3. Executive summary
4. The problem at first sight:
       The symptoms of the problem
       Why the client thinks there is a problem
       Where it hurts
5. The investigation:
       What we were called in to do
       What we did
6. The problem uncovered:
       What the roots of the problem are
       What the full extent of the problem is
       What happens if we let the problem continue
7. Recommendations
8. Implementation of the recommended strategy
9. Costs and benefits
10. Appendices: for bulk data, references, etc.

ADDITIONAL CHAPTERS TO THE MAIN REPORT

Notice that for the academic audience it is best to add three additional chapters to the main report.

Methodology

How you got at the data; why you did it this way; what the alternative methods would have been; what the problems were in practice; how you overcame them.

This section is important because the academic audience wants to see how competent a researcher you are for future projects.

Literature

There is already a body of knowledge relevant to the subject which you have tackled. What is it? How far does it help?

The academic audience wants to be sure that you did not approach the project as a totally uneducated beginner ignorant of the existence of the whole body of scientific knowledge.

Reflections

You've done it. Now stand back and reflect on your experience. What have you learned? With the benefit of hindsight how might you have done it differently and perhaps better?

You may also like to add 'Suggestions for further research'.

The oral presentation 14

You have a short time, usually 15 minutes, to stand in front of your audience and talk to them, telling them about your research and what you recommend they should do.

Standing in front of an audience may seem scary until you have done it a few times. Once you are on stage it is relatively unfrightening; it can even be a high, a good experience *provided that* you have done two things thoroughly before you go on stage: **preparation** and **practice**. Prepare the presentation thoroughly in advance. Have a practice run; then have a second practice run in front of a timekeeper and a friendly audience who will give helpful, frank, and honest feedback. Then have another practice run if you need it.

PREPARATION

So how do you present your recommendations and the evidence to support them?

At the first step in preparing for presentation, it is necessary to reorganize the material. There is a large volume of data, analyses, ideas, conclusions. Most of it will not be presented to the client. The following steps will help you to organize the oral presentation.

STEP 1: REORGANIZE THE DATA

1. *Aim: Client action*
   The entire purpose of your presentation is to persuade your client to act. What do you want the client to do as a result of your presentation?
2. *Client*
   Who is your client? To whom are you making the presentation? There may be several audiences. One audience may hear the oral

presentation. Several others may receive copies of the written report. It is important to know who you are talking to; that is, who you are trying to persuade. Your presentation has succeeded if those people take the action you want them to.

3. *Recommendation*

   What do you recommend they should do? That is the key to all your presentations, written and oral. Build your presentations around that.

4. *Evidence*

   What is the evidence to support your recommendation? What are the key facts? Test them. Are they reliable? Destruction test them. Do you really believe them? You may need to go and collect some additional data to be sure.

   Remember that on your recommendation your client will take major decisions. Do not be tempted to overstate the evidence. Tell it like it is. Your client has the absolute right to rely on the information you give. If the information is not 100% reliable, say so.

5. *Pay-offs*

   If your proposal is accepted and acted on, what will be the outcome? What will be the costs and benefits to the client? The implied question for the client is: Why should I do this? What's in it for me? At its most basic, if we adopt your strategy, do we make more profit?

6. *Implementation*

   The strategy or proposed course of action has yet to be fitted into the existing company. To make the strategy work may require some additional changes. What are they?

When you have worked through these questions you are in a good position to begin designing the oral presentation (and the written reports). The answers to these preparatory questions are all you need for the presentations. The rest of the data heap can be set aside. That has probably consigned 80% of your papers to a storage file, making the rest much easier to handle.

STEP 2: PREPARE THE STORYLINE

The storyline is the logical structure of the oral presentation. Typically it begins with the research question, ends with the answer to that question, i.e. the recommendation. In between comes the essential evidence that leads the listener from question to answer. The flow of the logical structure and the evidence is so smooth and convincing that the audience arrive at the answer for themselves before you do. As a result, it is their answer and they are pleased with themselves when you confirm it. That may be an exaggeration, but with a purpose of explaining the aim of a storyline.

Example 5: Storyline format

THE QUESTION
leads to
THE EVIDENCE
leads to
THE ANSWER

Example 6: A storyline

1. We have investigated why our products are not selling well in Holland.
2. Our prices are competitive.
3. But they are not well known nor well marketed.
4. Consequently, potential customers do not believe that our after sales service will be as good as that of the more well-known competitors.
5. The problem stems from operating only through an agent, who has little commitment or motivation to develop the market for our products.
6. *Conclusion:* To develop the market would require a local subsidiary to be established in Holland.
7. *Recommendation:* Evaluate the profitability and feasibility of establishing a Dutch subsidiary either by acquisition or by starting from scratch.

The storyline tells the full story. It begins with the question. It ends with the answer to that question. In between are the keypoints which lead the listener from question to answer. Five or six points are all we have time for in a presentation which must hold the listeners' attention.

The storyline is **NOT** the presentation. It is part of the preparation. The storyline serves to put the essential information identified in Step 1 into a logical format for presentation.

STEP 3: DESTRUCTION TEST THE STORYLINE

1. *The question*
   - Is this the question that the audience expects to hear answered?
   - Does it capture their attention?
   - Is it of major importance to them? *NB: The question here is not whether it* **should** *be of importance to them, but* **will** *it be of riveting importance to them, the way you have phrased it?*]

2. *The key points A, B, C, D*
   - What are they?
   - Do they follow logically from one to the next?
   - Can you prove them?
   - Do they stand up to scrutiny?
   - How best to **show** each point?
   - Work through each point and test it for reliability.
   - Can you stand on it?
   - Will it support the weight you hope to put on it?
   - How best to get the point into your client's head?
3. *The answer*
   - The conclusion that all this has been leading up to.
   - You have posed a question.
   - The audience are interested in knowing the answer.
   - You have held their interest.
   - Now deliver.
   - *WHAT DO YOU RECOMMEND?* Does it follow as the logical and inevitable conclusion of all that has gone before? Or is it
     - genuine?
     - honest?
     - trustworthy?
     - credible?
   - Destruction test it.
   - How will the opposition shoot it down?

STEP 4: FIND THE BEST WAY TO COMMUNICATE YOUR MAIN POINTS TO THE LISTENERS

- How to prove your points, simply and effectively?
- How to illustrate them?
- Keep it brief, to the point, effective.

Here you can use pictures, graphs, visuals to make each of your key-points come alive. Remember that your presentation takes place in your audience's head, not on the screen.

STEP 5: PUT IT ALL TOGETHER AND SEE HOW IT WORKS AS ONE PRESENTATION

You may have to fine tune, adjust the balance, shorten it. You may find that all your visuals are clumped together in one half of the 15-minute programme and need readjusting.

Play with it until you are happy with it, confident that it works for the audience as well as for you.

Example 7. A storyline

Point 1. We have been asked by Petit Bateau, manufacturer of upmarket French children's clothes, how it should enter the UK market.

Point 2. Petit Bateau, as a proud family firm, is concerned to protect the very upmarket brand image, to avoid borrowing, and maintain high margins and a certain exclusivity.

Point 3. There are a number of possible ways to enter the UK market, such as own-label for Marks and Spencer, or national mass distribution through the national chain stores.

Point 4. These would have some attractions such as high volumes, but all would contradict key Petit Bateau objectives such as avoiding debt capital and maintaining brand image.

Point 5. *Recommendation*. We therefore recommend that Petit Bateau sell in the UK through Harrods and through selected upmarket boutiques and shops of that standard.

Important points to note

The storyline summarizes many months of hard work during which the team interviewed scores of store buyers, walked hundreds of miles with briefcases full of kids' underwear, accumulated several tons of paper. The client does not need to hear any of that in the oral presentation. All that the client needs to hear is summarized in the storyline.

- The storyline follows from point to point, smoothly and logically like a good story. It all hangs together well.
- The storyline leads to the conclusion, the recommendation.
- This is not yet the presentation.

The storyline is the framework of the oral presentation. One can see now which of the key points need illustrating, which need some factual evidence to prove them, where graphics would help to focus the audience's attention. And so the presentation is built up around the storyline.

STEP 6: PRACTICE RUN

Do a complete, formal practice run of the presentation, but without an audience. This is the time to find out if it works, if the parts fit together smoothly, if the balance and emphasis are right.

Make whatever changes are necessary until all the team is happy. Do not compromise. Find a better way of doing it.

STEP 7: FURTHER PRACTICE RUNS

Practice:

- with a timer to get the timing right;
- with a friendly audience for helpful, frank feedback;
- in the room where the final presentation will be made to check that it works well there.

Prepare for questions. Prepare how you will handle them.

STEP 8: GO FOR IT

If you have prepared this thoroughly you will have the confidence to do a good job and enjoy it.

Conclusion 15

A project well done contributes to many clients. It solves a problem for a corporate client, adds to the stock of knowledge of the community, adds substantially to the capability and the confidence of the researcher.

If you have worked diligently through each part of this book you have already greatly increased the probability of success of any project which you tackle. And the more experience you gain the better you will become at solving major management problems.

Having reached the end of the book, let us reflect on why we started. The aim of the book is to help you with your management project. Now that you have worked through the book you are in a strong position to succeed with the present project.

Why do projects?
As a practice run for solving major management problems in the real world.

There is no shortage of major management problems in the real world. One of the effects of our fast-developing technologies and our world markets is that we get our management problems faster and on a greater scale. Companies in the USA, Japan, and throughout Europe are faced with the problem of how to cope with a supposedly Single European Market. New opportunities, new threats, and a need for new approaches on a Pan-European scale.

On a larger scale there are new management problems to be faced. How to make the European Community work effectively? What will become of the old communist bloc of Eastern Europe? As millions of refugees move west to escape the economic collapse of the old Eastern bloc, how should the West, and particularly the EC, respond? Yugoslavia is slowly being partitioned along religious lines which follow the dividing line between Christianity and Islam in the Middle Ages. How do we manage that situation to the good of all parties? How do we remove starvation from Africa?

We have the management problem-solving processes to cope with such problems. They are precisely the same processes which we have used with any management research project. The purpose of the project, remember, is to teach you how to solve an unfamiliar problem whose answer is not known in advance. You are not required to know the answer before you start. You are learning how to investigate and understand the problem and how to find a good solution. It can be done if we choose to do it.

Part of the art, here as everywhere, is to identify the clients and know how to take them with you in pursuit of the good solution. Owning the problem is an important step towards solving it.

Let us reflect a while on what you can now do. You know how to solve complex, major management problems whose solution at the outset is unknown. That allows you to do many things. You know how to tackle problems for a company and how to lead a team to solve company problems. The range of opportunities to which this process can be applied is very wide; from moving into a new market, to acquiring and absorbing a new subsidiary, to diagnosing and remedying an outbreak of problem symptoms anywhere in the group. At the consulting and teaching level you now have the essential process skills on which most management consultancies thrive, and which made millionaires of researchers such as Porter, Peters, Waterman and many others. On a global scale you know how to go about finding a cure for famine in Africa and the EC Common Agricultural Policy. You may not have a ready-made solution at hand, but you do not need one. Given a client, support, and the political will to find a solution, you know how to find a solution.

You have a very powerful set of tools and understanding of the means to solve major management problems. Your skill in using them grows with each experience of tackling projects. How you will use them is up to you. It is always your choice. There is much that needs doing. Few are as well prepared as you to do it. If you who are able do not tackle the most important problems, one wonders who will. May you always be blessed and guided in your efforts. I wish you success, for the sake of all your clients and yourself.

Appendix
Project ideas

Wherever there is something that we do not know but would like to know, there is a research project. Since management is the art and science of getting things done, of making it happen, many of our most insistent problems can be tackled as management problems. For anyone seeking a research idea the possibilities are rich and varied. Here are almost two hundred project ideas. Each of them, if you think it over for a while, may suggest several other possible projects closer to your own interests.

These projects come from a wide variety of sources, companies, countries, and business schools. Project ideas have been chosen from the City University Business School, London, UK; Ecole Européenne des Affaires, Paris, France; ESCP, Paris, France; EAP, Madrid, Spain; EAP, Berlin, Germany; LUISS, Rome, Italy; the Universities of Bruxelles, Liege, Leuven, and Ghent in Belgium; the Universities of Oklahoma and California, and Harvard Business School in the USA.

The companies which have provided project ideas include: Citizen Watches of Japan; American Express; Coca Cola; Norwich Union; Prudential; Sun Alliance; Lloyds Insurance; AMEC PLC; Sainsbury; National Westminster Bank; J. Rothschild; Merrill Lynch; Nomura; National Farmers Union; Austin Rover; Skandia; Rhone Poulenc; and many others, to whom much thanks.

These project titles and ideas are presented here as a source of possible ideas and inspiration for the reader.

- Europe 1992 and transnational television: advertisers and Pan-European advertising.
- Future prospects and strategies for international accountancy companies in Europe with special emphasis on changing local conditions.
- The export consultancy sector in the UK, France, and Germany:

the skills, strategies and resources required to develop a successful practice.

- The internationalization of management consultancies. The case of Europe.
- Financial mergers: globalization versus niche market strategies. The British, German, and French experience.
- Mergers and acquisitions: procedures and strategies in the UK, Germany, and France. A comparative study.
- Mature industry restructuring: the European experience in shipbuilding.
- Buyer and supplier relationships in companies with Just-in-Time (JIT) production processes.
- Different trading methods for pharmaceutical multi-nationals in the ASEAN countries.
- Developing an integrated IT system for management decision making in a chemical company.
- Ditto for a management consultancy company.
- How to market banking services across Europe after 1992.
- Creating a market intelligence system covering the Single European Market.
- A review of treasury management theory, techniques and best practice, and their application to an international company in fast-moving consumer goods.
- How to develop a pan-European market strategy for a Japanese watch company given different market positions already established in Germany, Italy, and the UK.
- What do American employers really think of the MBAs graduating from American business schools?
- The ideal division of responsibility and decision making between the American head office and the European operating companies of a food and drink group.
- The role of learning in strategic management.
- The market for construction management services at Heathrow airport.
- Manpower planning arrangements at the BAA SE airports.
- Post completion audit of capital expenditure projects.
- A product lifecycle for the International Stock Exchange (London).
- A review of job analysis and appraisal attributes within the International Stock Exchange (London).
- Review of the 'Companyfile' Product – developed and sold by the International Stock Exchange.
- Feasibility study into a new distribution channel for the American Express Card.

- Creating a new distribution channel for the American Express Personal Card.
- Planning a new business startup.
- Career management in J. Sainsbury PLC.
- The use of the simulation technique for strategic management education.
- The identification of the marketing gap for providing an outplacement counselling service.
- A commercial appraisal of Basingstoke Cheese Department.
- Customer provider relationships in J. Sainsbury PLC.
- The use of a Homebase guarantee as a marketing tool.
- The changing role of IT within J. Sainsbury PLC.
- Occupational health care at J. Sainsbury PLC.
- Order Routing Management Systems: their strategic importance to the ISE.
- Product evaluation of uPVC windows: a cost benefit analysis approach.
- Improving financial management in the public sector.
- The formation and subsequent operation of a marketing department in Petrolite Ltd.
- Total Quality Management (TQM) in Petrolite Ltd.
- Financial systems and control: a strategic review for the 1990s.
- Departmental design and development: a guide for practising managers.
- Corporate culture in X PLC: What is the potential for fusion between the two main subcultures in the organization?
- 'Know Thyself': a study of the marketing potential of corporate identity and a model for the realization of individual and corporate identity for myself and X PLC.
- An analysis of J. Sainsbury PLC. Diversification strategy with particular reference to Homebase and the DIY market.
- Vision to action: effective team-building in a role culture.
- Gilt market strategy.
- The marketing of Taurus.
- Total Quality Management: implementation through people.
- Effecting strategic and cultural change at Rover – becoming a 'Build to Order' company.
- A management development programme for Allied Dunbar's south east region.
- Electronic mail: a strategy for Homebase.
- Developing financial services business from solicitors.
- An analysis of pre-registration marketing within the pharmaceutical industry.

- Manpower planning: an analysis of recruitment and retention in the retail division.
- An investigation into the concepts of total quality management on behalf of Prudential Portfolio Managers Ltd. Property Division.
- A manager's guide to change – the Norwich Union experience.
- How to make the most out of Information Technology to improve our business.
- The regionalization of the annuity departments: the management of change.
- An analysis of personal insurance customers requirements, attitudes towards insurance and images of insurance companies.
- Maximizing staff motivation (the interlinking between vision and motivation).
- Understanding cultures: a key to business successes.
- Development of electricity pool bidding strategy for a UK electricity generator.
- How the clearing banks can develop EDI to complete the paperless trading cycle.
- Contracting out IT and Telecom in a multi-national company.
- What privatization means to the customer.
- The Channel Tunnel – will shareholders ever see a return on their investment?
- Problems and opportunities for the London insurance market arising from the move to a Single European Market.
- The effect on the UK retail industry of full membership of the EMS and 1992.
- Strategic review of Lowndes Queensway collapse.
- Coloroll Group PLC – from initial public offering to corporate receivership.
- The search, acquisition, and strategic management of a company by a management buy-in team.
- Take three banks – a comparative assessment of the strategy of three British merchant banks, from 'Big Bang' (1986) to the Single European Market (1992).
- Business issues facing small information technology companies operating in the European financial sector.
- Investment opportunities in Eastern Europe.
- Developing an international business policy for Gallaher.
- Trading behind the Iron Curtain.
- Is it time for an affordable, non-polluting, recyclable automobile? A feasibility study and business plan.
- Estate agents – a strategy for the nineties.
- Alternative methods of small company finance, post–1991.

- The role of bonds in the financing of property development in comparison to conventional variable rate debt.
- Short-term interest rate risk management.
- The operation of securitization in the UK and future trends in domestic secondary loan markets.
- Business plan for the establishment of a green fund.
- The treasury role in a multi-national company – BP's perspective.
- Strategic business development of a small management buy-out.
- Fragmentation of the ethical pharmaceutical industry: Why and will it be overcome?
- The future evolution of British Rail.
- A new Europe – opportunities and threats. A study of the impact of changes in European financial regulation on UK financial institutions.
- Starting-up a new type of consultancy business – a feasibility study.
- The development of market economies in Eastern Europe – a business perspective.
- The UK venture capital industry: the changing face of the industry and strategies likely to be successful in the future.
- Use of commodity markets to manage developing countries' debt.
- Facing up to the future. Development of strategic planning within the London Futures and Options exchange.
- Practical implications and applications of arbitrage theory for bond, interest rate and foreign exchange markets in the financial institutions in those markets.
- Is there such a thing as an appropriate level of IT within an organization? Do a Formula One company, a gas sensors manufacturer and a publishing company have the solution?
- How do you measure the advertising effectiveness of insurance companies?
- Techniques in commodity price risk management for developing countries.
- The UK waste management industry – a strategy for the next decade.
- The management of companies in recession.
- A comparison between the real and theoretical composition and performance of a fund of funds using efficient market and modern portfolio theory analysis of the underlying subcomponent funds.
- Option-based analysis of convertible bonds and its application to the Korean Overseas CBS.
- The Arab as a consumer – a springboard for marketing in the Gulf States.
- Changing the rules of the game. The economic consequences of the Thatcher regime. A provisional assessment.
- Analysis of a new business development.

- Strategy and its implementation: Business Partners – International Dollar Card – Europe.
- Strategy and operating plan for CBO for 1992–1994.
- 'Total Quality Management' applied to the formulation of an application for Certification of Operations to BS 5750.
- A retrospective analysis of two major British Telecom logistics projects, with respect to existing project management methods.
- Lloyd's Underwriting – how to make the most of information technology to improve our business.
- Creating a contingency plan for the 1990s for a Lloyds insurance syndicate.
- Design a managerial strategy for internal audit.
- European cross border mergers and acquisitions in the Single Market – strategies and organizational capability.
- Does the European Currency Unity (ECU) offer strategic and marketing potential for the equity business of County Natwest?
- The line manager's role in developing people.
- The management of redundancy: corporate redundancy and the response of redundant managers.
- Building up a consultancy business from a polytechnic base.
- To research and introduce a strategy for management training and development for Irish Life UK.
- To formulate and evaluate options within the framework of developing a marketing strategy for Iron Trades Health Care for 1993/1994.
- The development of a career familiarization programme for implementation into London region.
- The role of a financial planning service in IRA's marketing strategy.
- Managing conflicts of interest within a multi-service financial organization: The Way Forward.
- Relating quality measurement and assurance to J. Sainsbury PLC software developments.
- An investigation into the costs and benefits of the introduction of a Sainsbury's 'customer loyalty' card and electronic marketing.
- The Sainsbury product strategy through the 1990s into the year 2000.
- Product and information networking and communication in J. Sainsbury.
- To study the alternative methods for building procurement for J. Sainsbury.
- How should management structure be developed in J. Sainsbury PLC to maximize the effectiveness of the senior branch management teams?
- How should information be received at the branch for senior management teams to (a) maximize information technology; (b) reduce paperwork; (c) get things done?

- Information technology will continue to play an ever-increasing part in the style of branch managing in J. Sainsbury PLC. What do you predict the change will be by the turn of the century?
- Human resource implications for the meat division of J. Sainsbury in the 1990s.
- Reward and incentive schemes in relation to quality requirements of shop floor employees.
- Designing and building an organizational framework which will enable the successful delivery of IS/IT to serve the store development business activities of a major food retailer.
- Team building for a German market.
- Managing schools – a framework for assessment quality.
- The link between poor housing and health.
- An exploration of the management development of women in SSD and its impact on the community.
- The development of the Juvenile Justice Service.
- Childcare planning.
- Marketing strategy for language service in the London Borough of Ealing: a model for local authority services.
- Marketing the Merrill Lynch Option Exercise Programme on a corporate basis.
- Marketing acute hospital services.
- The role of non-executive directors on the Board of an NHS Trust.
- Building a sales team.
- Managing conflicts of interest within a multi-service financial organization: the way forward.
- Quality service requirements in a changing market for insurance.
- Solicitors and financial services – the development of the legal profession as a distribution channel for financial services products.
- Implications of demographic and social changes for Norwich Union's marketing strategy.
- The analysis of customer needs and requirements in relation to personal insurance products.
- To examine the motivational options when managing people through a period of uncertainty.
- Market share: a strategy for commercial insurance.
- To improve the effectiveness of the working relationship between the management services division and unitized pensions division of the Norwich Union Group.
- Branding in a European context for an insurance company expanding its European market share.
- Effective team working: a framework for development.
- The management MBA at Norwich Union – great expectations?

- Provide NU with a formal, maintainable IT strategy consistent with the business plan.
- Feasibility of reinforcing the core values within NU by linking them to the reward system and make recommendations.
- Corporate planning for Norwich Union Schadeverzekering NV.
- Marketing strategy for Norwich Union Schadeverzekering NV.
- An investigation into the role of TQM within insurance companies.
- A review of computer security risks.
- Enabling a 'cultural change' in Rover to a 'build to customer order company'.
- Rover's developing collaborative partnership with Honda: an appraisal of the venture's 'fit' in relation to Honda and Rover business strategy.
- Measuring advertising effectiveness in the automobile industry.
- To embody the 'learning' concept in the direction and application of the Rover Groups.
- Marketing strategy for armour protected saloon cars.
- A business strategy for the sustained profitable expansion of the Sun Alliance accident portfolio through the 1990s.
- Management of change within Protea with the installation of a new IT system.
- Devise a strategy for the development of financial risks insurance products globally.
- Development of a model defining the appropriate information needs of key decision-makers within an NHS region with whom the pharmaceutical industry must interact.
- An analysis of pre-marketing within the UK pharmaceutical industry.
- Organizational change within a pharmaceutical marketing group.
- Use of information technology to provide competitive edge in marketing pharmaceuticals.
- Developing a business plan for West London TEC.
- Developing a marketing strategy for West London TEC.
- Developing a MIS strategy for West London TEC.

Bibliography

Ackoff, R. (1978) *The Art of Problem Solving*, John Wiley, Chichester.

Blalock and Blalock (1968) *Methodology in Social Research*, McGraw Hill, New York.

Bryman, A. (1989) *Research Methods and Organisation Studies*, Unwin Hyman, London.

Clark, P. (1979) *Action Research and Organisational Change*, Harper & Row, New York.

Cova, B. (1989) *La Recherche en Gestion*, EAP, Paris.

Cumberlidge, P. (1978) PhD Thesis, University of Bath.

Easterby-Smith, Thorpe and Lowe (1991) *Management Research*, Sage Publications, London.

Eden, C. and Sims, D. (1977) *Problem Definition Between Clients and Consultants*, University of Bath.

Frost, P. and Stablein, R. (1992) *Doing Exemplary Research*, Sage Publications, London.

Gay, L.R. (1990) *Educational Research*, Macmillan Publishing, New York.

Harre, R. and Secord, P. (1972) *The Explanation of Social Behaviour*, Blackwell, Oxford.

Hempel, C. (1972) *Elements d'Epistemologie*, University of Paris.

Hofstede, G. (1981) *Culture's Consequences*, Sage Publications, London.

Jankowicz, D. (1991) *Business Research Projects for Students*, Chapman & Hall, London.

Jay, A. (1985) *Effective Presentation*, BIM.

Jung, C.G. (1958) *The Undiscovered Self*, Routledge, London.

Jung, C.G. (1971) *Psychological Types*, Routledge, London.

Lofland, J. (1976) *Doing Social Life*, Wiley, New York.

Markides, K. (1990) *The Magus of Stravolos*, Penguin, Harmondsworth.

Markides, K. (1991) *Fire in the Heart*, Penguin, Harmondsworth.

Miller, J. (1983) *States of Mind*, BBC Books, London.

Peters, T. and Waterman, R. (1982) *In Search of Excellence*, Harper & Row, New York.

Porter, M. (1985) *Competitive Advantage*, Free Press, New York.

Porter, M. (1980) *Competitive Strategy*, Free Press, New York.

Popper, K. (1972) *Objective Knowledge*, Clavendon Press.

Raimond, P. (1986) PhD Thesis, University of Bath.

Reason, P. and Rowan, J. (1981) *Human Inquiry: A Sourcebook*, Wiley, New York.

Rogers, C. (1961) *On Becoming a Person*, Constable, London.

Rudestam, K. and Newton, R. (1992) *Surviving Your Dissertation*, Sage Publications, London.

Schein, E. (1969) *Process Consultation*, Addison Wesley, Wokingham.

Stevens, A. (1990) *On Jung*, Routledge, London.

Storr, A. (1974) *Jung*, Fontana, London.

Wilhelm, R. (1951) *I Ching*, Routledge, London.

Wilhelm, R. and Jung, C.G. (1931) *The Secret of the Golden Flower*, Kegan Paul, London.

Index